Dean Hoge
Patrick McNamara
Charles Zech

Final Chapter by Loren B. Mead

Plain Talk
about
churches
and
MONEY

An Alban Institute Publication

Library of Congress Catalog Card Number 97-73982
ISBN 1-56699-185-4

CONTENTS

FOREWORD

This book should get people talking! It is about one of the most popular, tantalizing, scandal-ridden, and dangerous subjects in contemporary life: money. Choose any day, and it's a safe bet that you cannot pick up a newspaper or watch a TV newscast that does not feature a big money story. This corporate takeover, that governmental tax cut, this spectacular family fight over the direction of a corporation, this embezzlement, that theft or, as the white-collar folks like to put it, misappropriation. Money touches everything—sports, the arts, certainly politics, charity, even religion.

So why won't this book about money be an instant megaseller like those that tell us how to become millionaires through the stock market, real estate, or some get-rich-quick scheme? Why won't it be cocktail party fodder like the latest expose on the spending habits of someone who is a candidate for Robin Leach's list of the rich and famous?

It's that word "churches" in the title. To be sure, churches can make headlines about money. With stunning regularity American religion produces one Elmer Gantry after another. Sharp-eyed journalists produce page-turners about the dark side of the money-and-church beat. Those who study philanthropy regularly remind us that churches still receive the largest share of charitable dollars. Denominations and congregations possess vast wealth—no one really knows what the real estate holdings, art treasures, and investments portfolios add up to. So big stories about money and the churches can be told. Big stories about tremendous economic creativity and enterprises that do justice and show mercy. And, sadly, big stories about irresponsibility, waste, fraud, and outright theft.

Plain Talk about Churches and Money is not one of those potboilers. Instead, this book seeks to provide useful information to church leaders who must deal with the financial realities that accompany modern life. *Plain Talk* holds up a mirror to the ways we raise money, manage it, and think and talk about it. Those who direct stewardship campaigns, serve on investment committees, plan budgets, and lead religious institutions will benefit from looking in this mirror. So will those who wish to motivate others to support the ministries of our congregations with their dollars.

Dean Hoge and Patrick McNamara are sociologists, and Charles Zech is an economist. All three get paid to describe what is really happening in the world. This book will not tell anyone what the latest hot fund-raising gimmick is. Instead, *Plain Talk* seeks to help us understand what we are doing, why some things we do work, and why others don't. So get ready to listen in as clergy talk about their own experience in the world of congregational stewardship. Readers will learn why some clergy cannot imagine working in a situation where they do not know what their members give. You will also hear why others refuse to learn that sensitive information.

If we look carefully into this mirror, we will find that one of the reasons money is so hard to talk about in the churches is that clergy carry deep personal ambivalence about this topic. This is one of the most painful areas of pastoral life–a place where resentments, anger, and great disappointment lurk. The plain talk in this book confronts the fact that clergy are unprepared for the fiscal responsibilities of their roles. The plain talk reveals clergy's great fear of the laity, and exposes the ways clergy and lay people collude to create a thundering silence about money in most of our churches. We talk about money only when we have to; we are ill at ease when we must get down to bottom lines; and we handle this topic with an amazing variety of kid gloves. In this book, we invite you to join the debate, to feel the ambiguity of being both a spiritual and financial leader.

In another chapter you will consider the variety of motivations people have for giving–and learn that many people give for reasons very different from those preached in stewardship sermons. Again, enter the conversation with the various points of view described here. Should secular fund-raising tactics be used in religious institutions? How do we help people drowning in a flood of fund-raising appeals respond to the different motivations religious communities seek to nurture? How do we live in the tension between the needs to raise money to keep our religious institutions afloat and to teach a distinctive way of caring for the world and responding to God's grace?

Read on. Consider the main money-raising strategies used by congregations—tithing, pledging, fall stewardship campaigns, and the like. Are they adequate to our age? Do we need to reclaim old strategies and patterns, or should we accommodate ourselves to the realities of late American capitalism and reach for the latest successful fund-raising techniques? Either way you answer, remember that the competition for each charitable dollar is only going to multiply. As you ponder these questions, take advantage of one of the book's greatest strengths: its comparative approach. Place your own practices and beliefs alongside those of denominations and congregations like your own and different from yours.

So why, if the topic is so sensitive, are we publishing a book that doesn't fall into the expose mold? Because the missions of our congregations require that we be creative and faithful users of money. Because we need basic information about this side of our religious life. *Plain Talk* invites you to pull up a chair and become early partners in a much needed conversation about faith and money. I imagine each chapter could serve as a discussion starter among various groups in our congregations. Stewardship committees, vestries and boards, clergy groups, and adult education classes could all use sections of *Plain Talk* to set off constructive talk in their home congregations.

This book is the first in the Money, Faith, and Lifestyle Series, which The Alban Institute will produce over the next few years in the hope that we can help congregations talk and think about money in more effective and faithful ways. Our series also intends to help congregations develop better ways to manage money, to raise it, and to build venture capital for ministry. We invite you to become pioneers who cross the invisible but very real membrane that keeps church people, clergy and members alike, from talking well about one of the most important realities facing them in their daily lives and in their congregational settings: money. I invite you to stay with us as the conversation unfolds in several directions. Think of ways to invite others to add their voices. Keep us posted on what you are learning.

James P. Wind

ACKNOWLEDGMENTS

This book could not have been written without the support and coopera-tion of a large number of people. We would like to thank them.

We had the privilege of interviewing many clergy who opened their minds and hearts to us. They provided us with their experiences, their insights, their "plain talk about churches and money." There were far too many for us to name all of them here, but we would like to express our special gratitude to the Rev. Ron Bruckner, the Rev. John Sharp, the Rev. Theodore Schneider, the Rev. John Stephens, the Rev. Edward White, the Rev. Mary Krause, the Rev. Dick Wohlschlaeger, the Rev. Randy Williamson, and the Rev. Frederick Stevenson.

Three people took the time to read a draft of this book and provide us with their honest feedback. They were the Rev. Elizabeth Carl, the Rev. Robert Craig, and the Rev. Chris Hobgood. This book is better because of their effort.

The staff at The Alban Institute were a delight to work with. James Wind, the president of The Alban Institute, along with Loren Mead, Celia Hahn, and editor Beth Ann Gaede, gave us encouragement along the way. They also read early drafts of this book and provided us with invaluable guidance.

This book is partly a product of a larger study of American churches and money supported by the Lilly Endowment, Inc. We thank them for their help, especially for the encouragement of Fred Hofheinz, program officer for religion.

Dean R. Hoge
Patrick McNamara
Charles Zech

INTRODUCTION

Worries about fund raising and finances beset all church leaders. There is a kind of bottom line inevitability to finances because, when all is said and done, churches need contributions to continue. The money they have limits what they can do.

Worried commentators also abound. C. Kirk Hadaway and David Roozen in *Rerouting the Protestant Mainstream* write about today's "cooler climate" for church growth and support, particularly among the baby boomers.[1] They are echoed by Loren Mead who foresees a "financial meltdown" in the mainline denominations:

> I use the term . . . intentionally to suggest that something essentially irreversible has happened within the financial and organizational systems of the mainline denominations, and that the impact of this is only beginning to be felt. I see almost no response by denominational or institutional leadership that indicates awareness of the severity of the crisis.[2]

In their book *Behind the Stained Glass Windows*, John and Sylvia Ronsvalle report that giving in all Protestant denominations has been declining as a percentage of parishioners' income for several decades.[3]

We believe that empirical research on church giving can help to reveal a way out. Today there are numerous good books on the theology of stewardship. There are also good publications by consultants such as Kennon Callahan and Herb Miller that give almost day-by-day plans of how to carry out stewardship pledge drives and how to build up church endowments. But systematic social science research on church giving is lacking. The three of us dedicated ourselves a few years ago to filling that gap, and this book is one result.

We believe this book is unique in its empirical, "bring-'em-back-alive" approach, its preference for plain talk, and its lack of reliance on a single theological view. The three of us are social scientists, not theologians, but we have something to offer. Dean Hoge is Professor of Sociology at the Catholic University of America. Patrick McNamara is Professor of Sociology at the University of New Mexico in Albuquerque. Charles Zech is Professor of Economics at Villanova University. In past years all three of us have published books and articles analyzing American churches. All three of us are active laypersons in our churches, both Protestant and Catholic. In the last five years we have scoured the research literature on gift-giving, altruism, church finances, and organizational commitment. Most importantly, we have worked for several years on an empirical study of five denominations in the United States—Catholic, Assemblies of God, Southern Baptist, ELCA Lutheran, and Presbyterian (USA). The results were published in 1996 in our book *Money Matters: Personal Giving in American Churches*.[4]

In this book we rely heavily on the research that went into *Money Matters* because it was the most thorough study of church giving ever undertaken. Supported by the Lilly Endowment, it covered 625 congregations (125 from each of the five denominations). Pastors or their assistants filled out a report on the financial status of their churches, and almost 11,000 laypersons from these five denominations responded to questionnaires. Our questions asked about donations to one's local church, to one's denomination, to other religious organizations, and to nonreligious causes. Our study also included data from a nationwide Gallup Poll of 1,000 American churchgoers as well as case studies of four successful Catholic parishes and nine Protestant congregations.

We include in this book additional material from about fifteen interviews with experienced pastors as well as observations conducted by Patrick McNamara during a separate case study of strong stewardship churches in 1996. The case studies included visits to Sunday school classes and church services and informal visits with parishioners over coffee and donuts after church.

Our emphasis here is on mainline Protestant churches. Let us be clear, however: our research does not include *all* types of mainline churches. Very small churches, ethnic-based and immigrant-based congregations, and Black churches did not appear often enough in our sample to give us much information. Our interviews with pastors did not include pastors of small churches or ethnic churches.[5] Based on our experiences with the churches we *did* study, however, we will offer our conclusions and state why we arrived at them.

The account that follows will be free of academic references, jargon, and data tables. In footnotes we will list the main research studies on which we draw. Busy professionals have little time to search the results for themselves; we have tried to do that for you. Our account here will be as useful and as clarifying as possible.

We are fully aware of the blinders, hesitancies, and euphemisms that populate this realm of behavior. Sociologists have long known that what passes for reality in any group of people may as well *be* reality in terms of its consequences. That is, if people believe that something is real, they will behave accordingly. Beliefs about God and God's people are central here. The observer studying religious giving needs to know the real theological world view of the person(s) under study (not just the official theology of the denomination) because otherwise the observer has no hope of understanding the giving.

The real theological view of a person is not easy to know and cannot easily be assessed in interviews. In addition, in our present-day culture, people are often hesitant to speak their theological views in the presence of an outsider whose tolerance of these views is unknown. Therefore a researcher talking with people about religious giving finds himself or herself negotiating self-presentations and frames of reference. The person being interviewed—particularly a lay person—will look for clues that answer the questions, "Are you one of us?" "Do you understand me?" and "Do you affirm what I am saying?" Some church members will tell us what they think we want to hear; others will be hesitant to state their real opinions or to admit that their true religious views do not match those officially taught in the congregation.

We need to be clear about the distinction between theological statements and descriptive research. Research usually tries to be as reliable as possible and as free from theological bias as possible. It attempts to depict actual behavior and the actual conditions of life today, without making strong judgments about what is right and wrong. Our strength as social scientists lies in descriptive research, not theology, and we will be slow to make any theological judgments about what is better or worse, or what God really prefers.

This book is mainly about mainline Protestantism in the United States. It occasionally draws on Catholicism on the one hand, and on evangelicalism on the other. It does so for comparative purposes. But we are speaking mainly to Protestant mainline clergy and laity.

Many pastors and laity feel confused about financial topics. For example, we found endless confusion about the word *stewardship*. The word is used loosely today, sometimes meaning a theological way of life, sometimes meaning management of all resources available to a church, sometimes meaning fund raising. Our interest is in the broadest theological meaning, not just gathering money; it includes elements of spirituality and discipleship. We try to be clear about the different meanings of the word in use today.

We also found pervasive doubts among clergy and laity about whether churches as we now know them can survive in the future. People talked to us about the new paradigm churches, about the "end of Christendom," and about the transformations needed in institutional religion. This book treats topics about the future only in passing. The book is dedicated mainly to a depiction of the situation in churches today, and we must leave discussion of future innovations to others.

Plan of the Book

Chapter 1 concerns issues directly affecting clergy attitudes toward money and toward their own roles with regard to financial support of their churches. Chapter 2 reviews financial programs used by churches today, including the historical development of such programs. Chapters 3 and 4 explore the motivations for giving money to the church (that is, why give in the first place) and the issues related to these that arise in everyday church life. Chapters 5 and 6 examine stewardship programs and their basic elements such as distinguishing stewardship from fund raising, and the complexities of pledging, tithing, and budgeting. Chapter 7 discusses the management of invested funds and endowments. Chapter 8, written by Loren Mead, explores his own conclusions and lessons from the research. Chapters 1, 4, 5, 6, and 7 feature numerous verbatim quotations from veteran pastors, mostly mainline Protestants. Not all pastors see these issues the same way. We have chosen those we believe to be insightful and representative of clergy we talked to.

Readers who tire of these quotes can skip many of them because we have stated summaries of them in the text.

Each chapter in the book ends with several questions for reflection and discussion. Some of the questions are directed specifically at pastors, and others apply to both pastors and laity. All will be helpful in analyzing one's own church.

We believe these pages will be valuable to pastors, church staff members, and those many rows of Sunday attenders upon whom our churches crucially depend for support.

CHAPTER 1

Why Are Pastors Uneasy about Money?

We need to begin with some plain talk about pastors' attitudes towards raising money. If pastors are to lead their congregations' fund-raising efforts effectively, they must be comfortable with their own role. Yet many pastors feel anxious about church finances. And most people— not just pastors—shrink at the task of soliciting money, no matter how worthy the cause. John and Sylvia Ronsvalle, in their book *Beyond the Stained Glass Windows*, report that only 6 percent of the pastors they surveyed agreed with the statement, "Most pastors enjoy preaching about money."[1] In our experience 6 percent might even be an over-estimate! The pastors we spoke with shared some of the anxieties they and others feel about church finances.

The discomforts have several sources. One is that many pastors want to be liked by their church members, and they fear that they will alienate members if they push too hard on money issues. A related concern is that many pastors enter ministry in the first place because they want to maintain the primacy of spiritual over temporal matters. They worry that their message will get lost if they appear to be too preoccupied with raising money. Finally, there is the pastor's own financial situation. Many expressed concern to us about how their family financial circumstances, including their own giving to the church, impacts their ability to talk about money, as well as how their message is received by church members.

This chapter addresses each of these issues. It begins with pastors' comments about their own training, then takes up the sources of their uneasiness.

Seminary Training

The pastors we talked with had definite opinions about their seminary training in church finances. They were unanimous: seminary training had prepared them poorly. This agrees with the survey of pastors reported by John and Sylvia Ronsvalle in which only 9 percent said that they had received adequate training about the financial aspects of churches during seminary.[2] One older Presbyterian pastor told us the following:

> I called up a man the other day and asked, "When are you retiring?" And he said, "I've got just two more stewardship drives to go and it's over!" That was his measure! Stewardship *consumes* these guys but it was never touched on in seminary, at least it wasn't forty years ago.

A United Methodist pastor concurred:

> To be perfectly honest with you, I think many in my generation of seminary training never really focused on this aspect of church membership. I guess we used the one vow that talked about giving time, talent, and gifts to the church and we left it ambiguous. . . . The ABCs of raising money for a budget, or raising money for endowment, or getting people turned on to the ABCs of giving to mission were never addressed.

He bemoaned his inadequate training.

> I regret that my generation missed a lot. I think I could have made a difference in some settings had I had some expertise in that area. You can't live on "what ifs" and "shoulds" and "coulds," but looking back now, that's the way I see it.

One pastor was not convinced that things have changed for the better in the seminaries. He feels they have gotten worse. When he was a young seminarian in the 1950s, he and most of his generation were taught by a seminary faculty comprised primarily of former pastors, who were "intellectually honest and good people, with pastoral experience."

He is critical of today's seminary faculty, who have little pastoral experience:

> Today, it's almost exactly the opposite. All of the faculty have gone the academic route. They've gone from seminary to graduate study to some sort of an internship, then back to the seminary. So today you don't have pastors or anybody with any kind of pastoral experience teaching in the seminaries. And I think that influences how those who are coming out as pastors feel on subjects like finances. If those guys who are teaching have not really had to produce funds and have not had to deal with a congregation, they aren't going to talk to them about this.

A Lutheran denominational leader guessed that pastors' anxieties over their perceived inadequate training in financial issues will probably get worse. This is not because of poor seminary training. Rather, it is because the technical aspects of raising money are growing more complex:

> I think that we have to acknowledge that there's a lot of anxiety and depression out there among the pastors. It has to do, I think, with a lot of changes that have come about in the relationship between the Christian faith and the secular world. You hear about Loren Mead and "transforming congregations for the future," and all the ideas and paradigm shifts that you have out there. You see the actual reality of people wanting to designate more, wanting to know exactly where their resources are being used and what's happening to them, rather than giving just to general support. You have a whole new thrust within the churches dealing not only with designated gifts, but also with planned giving, annuities, endowments, and all the rest. You have a changed set of attitudes about denominational leaders. It's all new, and it makes many pastors feel inadequate.

A 1991 survey of Catholic and mainline Protestant pastors looked into this topic. In telephone interviews, researchers asked the pastors if various parts of their ministry were relatively more, or less, satisfying. The pastors said that administrative and financial duties were the least satisfying parts of their ministry. They found their main satisfaction in pastoral and theological roles. Are the pastors satisfied with their ability and skills in administrative and financial management? Most said no. They said they never had good training; more than 85 percent said they were dissatisfied with the administrative and financial training they had received in seminary.

How about their interest in taking short courses and seminars on these topics now? Most pastors said they were not very interested. They told the researchers, in effect, that while administration and financial matters are important, they themselves did not want to take the lead on them. They would prefer to be left alone to exercise their theological, liturgical, and pastoral duties and to give management tasks to someone else.[3]

The same research project included a survey of academic deans and presidents of Catholic and Protestant theological seminaries. Do the seminaries teach financial skills? Most seminaries offer courses in management, leadership, and finances, but the courses are normally electives, not required. The seminary leaders were not convinced that they had a responsibility to teach these topics; about half said that the seminary curriculum is already filled up, and practical management skills need to be acquired later.[4]

Everyone we talked with said the same thing. Seminaries have done a poor job of training their students for the financial side of ministry. In defense of the seminaries, though, it should be noted that they are expected to cover a broad range of subjects in a short time, and church finances are not a high priority. Much of the training must be gotten later on the job.

Fear of Alienating the Laity

Money is an awkward topic to talk about. Pastors are human, and they want to be loved and respected by denominational leaders, by other clergy, and by the laity. In fact, most pastors *are* loved and respected. But they all hope to avoid situations in which they risk losing the love and respect of their parishioners. Asking for money presents such a situation.

It may be that pastors are as a group psychologically more influenced than average by the perceptions of other people. A Lutheran pastor who had some clinical training has observed the psychological profile of pastors:

> If you're a Myers-Briggs fan, the ENFJ/Ps tend to gravitate toward ministry—the people who are extroverted, intuitive, feeling, and judgers or perceivers. They tend to like to have the affirmation of other people. And that's pretty true of all the ministers I know. We wouldn't be in the profession or calling we are in, unless we really cared for and valued people *and* their affirmation for us.
>
> So having said that as a backdrop, when you go to people and say, "Okay, we've got to talk about money," most ministers I know are a little shy of that because they know that it can be a negative and confrontational subject for some folks. They just try to avoid it. "Don't get into that because when you get into that, it will mean conflict." I think a lot of ministers tend to avoid conflict. They don't like to see it coming. They like to see everybody happy. And they go to great lengths to see that that happens. And one of the ways you do it is, don't kick too hard on the money.

Other pastors confirmed that the need of pastors to be loved can be an impediment to developing a good fund-raising message. A Lutheran pastor in a self-reflective moment said:

> My commitment to stewardship was pretty good. But it was my need to please and my cowardice at challenging others to follow my example that was my problem.

A pastor who was critical of seminary training felt that seminaries reinforced the natural avoidance of pastors to risk offending by asking for money:

> I think too much teaching in seminaries has been what I call touchy-feely teaching: "Ah, you don't want to offend someone, you've got to help them." I don't know! I wasn't raised that way, and I'm not comfortable with it. For me, I don't *want* to offend you, but I'll tell you how I feel. I thought that's why you employed me.

As difficult as it is for pastors to talk about financial responsibility with the congregation as a whole, it is even more difficult to talk about it with close personal friends. How do you approach friends about their giving without offending them, especially if the pastor perceives that there is a problem with their financial commitment? An Episcopal priest was struggling with this when we spoke:

> I'm in the middle of that right now. My wife and I are good friends with a couple our age in the parish, and the bookkeeper told me they have cut back their pledge substantially. And I'm really upset about that, and I'm not sure what to do about that. I think what I need to do is say to them, "I understand from our bookkeeper that you have cut back your pledge. Is there something wrong you need to tell me about, or do you have a complaint here?" But I haven't done it because they're also good friends. But I need to do that.

Finally, one pastor referred to a "collusion between the laity and the clergy." In this pastor's experience, the laity are sending a signal to the clergy that "we don't want you to talk about money, and you don't want to, so let's not." The pastors are more than happy to engage in this conspiracy, and as a result nobody says more than is absolutely necessary. This person also felt that the issue may not even be about money alone. Money may merely be a front for other aspects of a Christian's life, such as faith, satisfaction with the church, or questions of economic justice. Pastors often do not want to get into these other issues.

Pastors want the love and respect of others, and naturally they avoid alienating their congregations. But they have a job to do. One of the crucial aspects of that job is that of helping people develop habits of stewardship, and as a byproduct ensuring the financial stability of the church. The task cannot be avoided. Somehow pastors need to find ways to be spiritual leaders and also financial leaders. They must develop an approach to church finances that helps church members grow in their stewardship commitment without alienating them.

Pastor Grabadollar

One fear felt by nearly every pastor is fear of the criticism, "You're always talking about money." For the vast majority of pastors, this criticism is unfair. Most pastors go to great lengths to *avoid* talking about money because they know how sensitive and potentially alienating it is. Yet the topic of money cannot be sidestepped. It continually appears in scripture readings in worship and it is a necessary topic at stewardship and budgeting time. The pastors we spoke with said that the attitude that all they talk about is money is sometimes heard in their churches, in spite of everything. It always hurts. A Lutheran pastor captured the sentiments of many:

> I came out of seminary very suspicious of financially self-aggrandizing clergy, and I tried very hard to maintain integrity for myself as a nonmercenary but stipendiary clergy (laugh). In fact, in my third parish I had a member who was quite a good stand-up comedian. And he did a cocktail party routine about a mythical "Reverend Grabadollar" that was hilariously done, but that struck fear in my heart, because I hadn't quite reconciled this thing for myself.

It does not seem to matter who is doing the asking or what the tone of the message is. An Episcopal priest related the reaction of a few of his parishioners to his parish's annual stewardship drive:

> In the fall for a couple of weeks we have laypersons stand up at the service and give a two minute talk about the importance of meaningful stewardship and why our budget needs help and needs people to take seriously what we are saying about stewardship. Still we had a couple of people say, "Week after week you are pounding us about money!"

One reason why many pastors are so sensitive to this issue is that they resent any possible comparison between themselves and televangelists. One Lutheran pastor said:

> I think the other part of it, unfortunately, is the association with people like Jim and Tammy Bakker and Jimmy Swaggart. And the people on TV who kind of have a huckster appeal. The pastors don't want to be associated with that.

Lee Strobel, in his book about the Willow Creek Community

Church megachurch, tells of the skepticism that Americans feel about preachers asking for donations.[5] He too feels that the television preachers have contributed to a wide distrust of all ministers in the area of finance. Strobel writes about the decisions at Willow Creek:

> Churches can defuse skepticism by being up front about their finances. For example, at our church if someone comes up to the visitor's center and asks questions about the church's expenditures, the volunteer immediately offers him a copy of the church's full financial statement, audited by an outside accounting firm.[6]

Strobel says that pastors can mitigate any unfavorable comparisons with televangelists by discussing finances openly, with accountability and integrity:

> It's critical that all churches understand that they are under scrutiny by Unchurched Harry and Mary. . . . How finances are handled is a litmus test for many of them.[7]

But it is not just the televangelists who create the distrust that makes the fund-raising tasks of pastors more difficult. It is also telemarketing. Rick Warren, pastor of the widely known Saddleback Valley Community Church, said that early in his ministry he was reluctant to teach about money and giving due to the pervasive cynicism among Americans about fund raising. Every day people receive appeals for funds in the mail that often use gimmicks. People are suspicious of fund raisers, and Warren did not want to get into the business. He told his people that God wants nothing to do with gimmicks and manipulation. Guilt, pressure, and hype have no place in God's work.

Lay leaders can be valuable in helping pastors overcome their fear of being seen as only interested in money. The Lutheran pastor who was scarred by the Reverend Grabadollar image told us how he overcame this fear.

> A big corporate executive from Pittsburgh Plate Glass on our church council once said to me, "Pastor, this congregation is never going to reach its goals until you take a more aggressive out-front position. We know how you feel. We'll protect your flanks. We

know your own stewardship and your own commitment. But we
need more out-front leadership from you." Well, with his support, I
sucked in my breath, rolled up my sleeves, and we raised the pledging in the fall campaign by 22 percent. That was a breakthrough
event in my life.

Related to the fear of being labeled Reverend Grabadollar is a basic
assumption held by many pastors. They see their ministerial task as being otherworldly rather than worldly. They want to serve their people on
a spiritual rather than temporal level. One Presbyterian pastor said:

> There's a sense among many pastors that they've been called into a
> spiritual realm, they've been called to be agents of the Lord. And
> they associate money and asking for money with the capitalist so-
> ciety and with the world. And a lot of them are uncomfortable. A
> lot of them are uncomfortable handling *their own* money. A lot are
> uncomfortable asking for money. It gets hooked up into salesman-
> ship and into fund raising, and a lot of them see it as being non-
> spiritual.
>   Some ministers pride themselves that they never even go to
> stewardship meetings. A minister who is otherworldly and sees
> himself or herself as being a spiritual agent of God and just wants
> to help people with care of their souls, may not even be very help-
> ful in raising money for the church.

We believe that the spiritual needs of the church members and the
temporal needs of the church organization need not be in direct conflict.
An authentic stewardship message requires that spiritual motivation be
basic to financial giving. An Episcopal priest said it this way:

> We are talking about your relationship with God. Before we even
> mention the word money, we are going to talk about what it means
> to know you have life as a gift. What does it mean to know that
> everything you have is a gift? What does it mean to know that the
> whole world is a gift of a gracious God? So I'm aggressive about
> that as a way of saying, "Do you know what I'm talking about? I'm
> not just asking you to give money. I'm talking about your spiritual
> life, which is what my job is." So that's how I deal with asking
> people for money.

Pastors' Personal Finances and Giving

A pastor's own personal financial situation can impact his or her attitude
toward money. It happens at several points. First is the reality that in
most congregations the pastor's compensation is a large portion of the
budget. Pastors who push hard during stewardship time may be seen by
others (or by themselves) as having a conflict of interest: "He's only
doing this to ensure that his own salary is secure," or "She's probably
pushing extra hard this year because her health insurance premiums went
up again." In their survey of pastors, John and Sylvia Ronsvalle asked if
this was a problem. Overall, 50 percent of the pastors agreed that the
fact that their salary was a large portion of the church's budget made it
difficult for them to preach about money. Their feelings varied by how
large their churches were. Almost 60 percent of the pastors of smaller
congregations (250 members or fewer) indicated that this was a concern
to them, but only about 45 percent of the pastors of larger congregations
(over 250 members) shared this concern.[8] Pastors of smaller churches
(whose salaries normally *are* a higher percentage of the budget) feel the
strain the most.

Should the pastor's compensation be clearly reported to the congregation? Would revealing that information have any impact on congregational giving? The pastors we spoke with were split on the question. The
Lutheran stewardship expert did not recommend reporting the pastor's
salary publicly:

> Well, I think it should be known within the leadership of the
> church, but I don't think as a general rule the salaries need to be
> published. It's better if they are not published. I think that people
> have a tendency to want *control*, and they use salaries as a control
> issue. I'm willing to let the spirit flow more. And rather than allow-
> ing people to use salaries as a control issue, I'd rather teach some-
> thing else.

Other pastors thought salaries should be public and did not mind. A
Presbyterian pastor reflected the views of many about revealing salaries:

> In the Presbyterian Church the congregation is required to approve
> the pastor's salary every year. In most budgets, personnel is a *very*

heavy part. And some of the comments you get are, "God, we're paying an awful lot of money for help around here." And we have to tell them what that help is doing. Like a lot of people, at first I winced and thought, "Oh my God, now they'll know." But the reaction I got from people coming out of church was, "Is that all you're getting for what you're doing?" That was the reaction I got (laugh).

A number of pastors talked about this question in a tone that revealed how sensitive it is. A United Methodist pastor was up front:

Very frankly, I hate to bang away at the church budget because if you sit down and look at a church budget for a church of our size and realize what percentage of the money that's raised goes to the pastor's salary, car expense, housing, insurance, and all the rest, it looks like you're beating the drum for your own cause. I have felt that way, especially at budget building time. I absolutely do not like to sit in on that piece of budget building. For me, I just feel uncomfortable when you realize how much goes for maintaining the pastor and the small percentage that we send to mission.

An Episcopal priest was scarred by a bad experience:

In the parish where I was before I came here, that happened, and it was a painful experience for me. It was a horrible experience for me. I had members of the vestry, in effect, decide that we really didn't need to raise more money since it was just to pay the pastor too much money.

Yet pastors are entitled to fair compensation. Some pastors are protected because the judicatory has established a salary scale based on congregation size and length of service, relieving them of the burden of negotiating their salary. In some churches we heard stories of the pastor's compensation showing up in pieces in different parts of the budget in order to hide the full amount and to deflect any criticism that the pastor's only concern is to raise enough money to pay his or her salary. Another approach is to adopt a "program-centered budget" or "goal-centered budget" that clearly indicates the allocation of each staff member's compensation (including the clergy's) to the various church programs. When confronted with this information, lay members are likely to be impressed by the amount and variety of the pastor's responsibilities, and perhaps less inclined to question the pastor's compensation. Pastors, when they see the same information, are possibly less inclined to feel guilty about the amount of their compensation.

Although the pastors we spoke with disagreed on whether salaries should be revealed, there was no disagreement at all on the importance of pastors giving generously themselves. It was unanimous. This is important because it removes a major worry. A Lutheran pastor saw other pastors' conflicts over their own giving as a major source of anxiety:

> They're scared to death of church finances. They see it as budget, and they're poor performers in giving themselves. They think, "I can't climb the pulpit steps and ask for a tithe if *I'm* not a tither." The people will know it, even if the financial records are locked up. The people will sense it. It's a lack of integrity.
>
> I believe you can't teach what you aren't. Pastors have to do it, they have to lay it on the counter and be open. Not because it is a prideful thing, but because no mountain was ever taken by any army with the guy bearing the flag at the rear. You just can't do it that way.
>
> Here in this church I can stand in the pulpit and preach tithing. And I know without a doubt that if somebody walks out the door angry because I turned the screws on them, there will be someone in this congregation who will say, "But he does it!" The oral tradition in the church will know that. Someone will say to that kind of person, "Right now the pastor is the major giver! He's not the major wage earner, but he's the major giver." And I know equally that if I were not a tither, I wouldn't get past the third sermon on that topic. I can't look you in the face and tell you to do what I'm not doing.
>
> You can't begin preaching financial responsibility until you're giving yourself. You've got to be a first person witness to the truth of what you preach.

Others would go even further. Besides believing that pastors need to be substantial givers to satisfy their own minds, they feel that pastors' monetary contribution should be public knowledge to establish their credibility in members' eyes. One Lutheran pastor spoke approvingly of a fellow pastor:

I once heard a guy say, "Here's how to run a campaign. You ought to stand up and say, 'This is what my wife and I are pledging.' "He was very much in favor of this approach. Say it up front: "This is what I'm going to give."

Not everyone agrees. When we asked a United Methodist pastor whether a pastor should state his or her level of giving, he thought for a moment and then replied:

I don't know. I really don't like that idea. I think it's too self-serving. That's just my gut reaction.

The pastors surveyed by John and Sylvia Ronsvalle agree with the United Methodist pastor quoted above. Only 37 percent agreed that church members would give more if they knew that their pastor was a tither, and only 18 percent thought that church members wanted to know what the pastor gave to the church.[9]

Last, there is the issue of the pastor's personal financial situation relative to the members. Pastors are professionals, and most have completed three years or more of graduate training after college. Like most students, they made (and asked their families to make) a financial sacrifice during those years, and many completed seminary training in serious debt. It would be natural for them to desire compensation comparable to that of other professionals such as doctors or lawyers who have made similar financial sacrifices for their education. In addition, many pastors find that their personal financial situation is well below that of the members of their congregation. They see that their members have homes and cars better than their own. If they are parents, their children play with friends from the congregation who have the latest electronic gadgets, more expensive clothes, more spending money, and so on.

Not all the pastors that we interviewed were sympathetic with pastors who are resentful because of their relatively lower income. Some cited the deep gratifications in ministry and the many side benefits of being a pastor. Others pointed out that pastors knew when they entered the ministry that they would not be drawing high salaries. A Presbyterian pastor had no sympathy with other pastors who pity themselves and contended that their salaries are not that low:

I have a real problem with that. It's not true in the Presbyterian
church. I just saw the published salaries of pastors. We're doing
pretty well, thank you. We have disposable income. Now, there's
a lot of pastors who love to whine and cry about money. But if you
wanted to make a lot of money, you shouldn't have been in the
ministry in the first place. My wife and I don't make a great
amount, either. Again, it's what you want to use it for. That's the
key question. It's disposable income.

An Episcopal priest had mixed feelings about his salary:

There are several things I could say. One is that I get paid fairly
well here. I get paid more than the average priest because I'm in
this parish which has a budget that is higher than the average parish.
So compared to other clergy, I'm fine. But living in this community, my family doesn't live like many families here do because we
live in the midst of two-career professional families. Every now
and then this gets to be a little bit of stress between my wife and I,
maybe.

A United Methodist pastor who had both a recent operation for
cancer and recent heart bypass surgery gave us a thoughtful response to
this question.

To be honest with you, it hasn't bothered me until very recently. I
know why it bothers me now. Physically, right now many people
would call it quits. Many people in my profession would say it's
enough. They say, "Why don't you just retire and do something
part-time?" That sounds awfully inviting, except the reality is it
would be very difficult to manage. In the next several years that
additional money that I can realize in the pension program and
social security will make a difference for me.
    It's in these moments that I get, not angry, I guess, but frustrated.
Then I realize that I felt called to this work, and the church was my
life from the time I was a kid on. I don't think I would have been
comfortable doing anything else, but I know that my wife and I are
going to be able to live in retirement on much less than most people
and still be happy and feel that life is fulfilling. I think about it. I

don't become angry about it. I made this decision with my eyes wide open.

We asked him if, given his financial situation, it bothered him that some congregation members are such poor givers. He hesitated, then replied:

> You want an honest answer? Yes! Recently this has been an issue for my wife and me because we are aware of some people who are really in a position to bless this church, and these are people who feel that the church is their lifeblood and they call upon every resource that we have and utilize it. I happen to know they always claim poverty and scrimping. I really have difficulty controlling my anger. I just think that, bless their hearts, if they knew what my wife and I are going to have to live on in retirement, they would be thankful that they have what they have and they would give to the church. I'm not going to change them, but yeah, it makes me angry.

To summarize, it is clear that many pastors find themselves conflicted over preaching about money. Their anxieties come from a variety of sources, as we have tried to describe. We believe that clergy can find some relief from many of these apprehensions. They can try to ground their message in sound theological and biblical roots. They can try to be open about their feelings. They can try to be exemplary givers themselves. They can educate themselves in financial matters.

We do not agree with pastors who think that money is nonspiritual or somehow evil. The Bible is full of discussions of money and possessions. A Lutheran pastor summarized the feelings of many others:

> The Bible is clear. In fact, in the scripture texts Jesus talked about money almost as much as anything else. He knew that the love of money, the courting of it, the praising of it, the worship of it, make it an idol of the first degree. He knew that it affected people's lives and how they approach God. I think my ministry colleagues know that, too. If we really do trust the word of God, we must know that Jesus talked about money a *whole lot*. And we *ought* to be biblical in asking for it. We shouldn't be afraid to ask for anything that helps do the will of God.

He continued:

I'm not sure it's all that much different between clergy and people. If clergy are excited about what they're doing, if people have a clear vision of what the church's program would accomplish, if they have a clear biblical perspective of what is promised, then I think these are successful programs. The clearer the better. The clearer biblically, the clearer in terms of the vision of what it's going to be used for, the clearer in terms of the promise of what happens when people give.

A final point must be made. Our interviewees made it clear to us that no matter how distasteful a pastor may find money discussions, he or she needs to have them. Stewardship is a part of ministry. A pastor cannot just say no. A Presbyterian pastor said:

Ministers need to take the lead. What if we had a minister who came to the session and said, "I'm a good preacher, but I just can't visit. So I'm not going to the hospitals and I'm not going to the homes to visit our people." We'd get rid of that person. The same is true of church finances. He or she *must* do it; they can't refuse. Especially in a capitalistic society. I think money and material things are so much a part of our milieu that the minister can't strike that area out for somebody else. We have to guide our people on how to use their money, how to give, how to run the church.

For Reflection and Discussion

1. What did you learn in seminary about stewardship? If you were to design a course on stewardship for today's seminarians, what would you put in the syllabus?

2. How do you think most lay people feel about stewardship sermons and appeals? Do your impressions about this affect your own feelings about providing leadership for stewardship matters? If so, how?

3. How do you feel about your own financial situation (including your

own level of giving)? How do your feelings affect your attitude toward your parish? your ability to talk to members of the congregation about their giving?

4. Do members of your congregation know what your salary and benefits are? Do they know how much you give to the church and others? Do you think they should know? Do you think changing your congregation's current practice in this matter would affect members' giving?

5. If you could change one or two things that would make it easier for you to teach and preach about stewardship and lead stewardship appeals, what would you change?

CHAPTER 2

Financial Programs Used by Churches Today

Let us look back at history for a moment. During most of Christian history since the conversion of Constantine in 312 A.D., churches were supported by taxes, land rents, and benefices. Throughout the Middle Ages, taxes and rents supported the institution. Freewill offerings from laity were marginal in importance; they were commonly deemed to be "alms" for helping the poor, not contributions for the basic costs of the institution. These arrangements changed with the French Revolution and the Napoleonic era, when most church lands in Europe were confiscated and clergy came to be supported by stipends from governments.

The American colonies started with the European system, but in the years 1750 to 1791, government tax support of Protestant congregations dwindled as ecclesiastical dissent spread. Dissenters objected to the virtual ownership of the churches by leading circles of people, and they urged total disestablishment of any church. By the time of the First Amendment to the Constitution in 1791, most congregations had disconnected themselves from any state financial support. The new method of church finances became pew rentals, and this slowly spread throughout the Protestant churches. Under this system, wealthy parishioners chose the best pews and sometimes rented extra ones for the poor to use.[1] To augment pew rentals, congregations often had collections, fairs, and various subscriptions. By the time of the Civil War, pew rentals were the standard method of financing, even though democratizing denominations such as the Methodists objected that the system discriminated against the poor and made them feel inferior.

Opponents of pew rentals sought better ways of financing congregations, ways that they hoped would reduce class distinctions. Some churches began advertising "all pews free." Gradually pew rentals were abandoned in favor of weekly offerings and pledge drives, supplemented by bazaars and fairs. By the 1920s pew rentals were generally abandoned in Protestant churches.[2]

Stewardship practices as we know them today date mainly from the 1910s and 1920s. These include the use of weekly envelopes, pledges, annual appeals, and canvassing of all members. Today pledging has become the major method of raising support in mainline Protestantism. Fund-raising projects such as fairs and bazaars provide small additional amounts, and groups within churches, notably women's organizations, often have their own projects and funds.[3] Some evangelical churches operate entirely on tithing, without any pledges. In all denominations, small churches tended to resist pledging, preferring to make informal annual appeals to heads of households. Jewish congregations took a different direction, and today they operate almost like social clubs, selling yearly memberships.

How Much Do Church Members Give?

Levels of giving to churches today vary widely by denomination. Some denominations have high levels, others low. Figure 1 depicts the variation in percentage of family income given annually; it shows amounts given by people who attend their churches at least once a year. At the top of the chart is the Church of Jesus Christ of Latter-Day Saints (the Mormons), followed by other recently founded Protestant religious movements—the Assemblies of God and the Seventh Day Adventists. The top part of the chart includes other theologically conservative groups such as the Southern Baptists. In the middle are the mainline Protestants, and at the bottom are the Catholics and two new small denominations, the Unitarian-Universalists and the Christian Scientists. In general, evangelicals and theological conservatives give more than mainliners, who in turn give more than Catholics.[4] Also in general (with a few exceptions), giving in America-founded denominations is greater than it is in denominations founded in Europe.

Figure 1 does not include the Jewish denominations. The reason is that Jews conceptualize their giving differently, thus for them the standard poll question (used for figure 1) is ambiguous: "About how

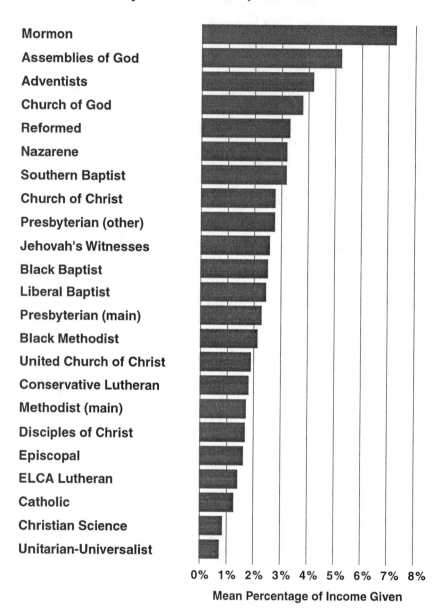

Figure 1

Giving as a Percentage of Income by Denomination, 1987-89

Denomination	
Mormon	
Assemblies of God	
Adventists	
Church of God	
Reformed	
Nazarene	
Southern Baptist	
Church of Christ	
Presbyterian (other)	
Jehovah's Witnesses	
Black Baptist	
Liberal Baptist	
Presbyterian (main)	
Black Methodist	
United Church of Christ	
Conservative Lutheran	
Methodist (main)	
Disciples of Christ	
Episcopal	
ELCA Lutheran	
Catholic	
Christian Science	
Unitarian-Universalist	

0% 1% 2% 3% 4% 5% 6% 7% 8%

Mean Percentage of Income Given

Source: General Social Survey, 1987-89. Persons who attend services at least yearly.

Based on data analysis by Stephen Hart.

Due to the small number of cases, figures for small denominations such as Adventists, Christian Science, and Unitarian-Universalist, are approximate.

much do you contribute to your religion every year, not including school tuition?" Jews give a higher percentage of their family income to Jewish causes (both religious and ethnic) than do Christians to Christian causes, and because their family incomes average about 1.5 times as high as the average for Christians, the total amount given is much higher.[5] But many of the donations are given to Jewish federations and appeals that are secular rather than religious, and the question "About how much do you contribute to your *religion* every year?" is unclear to Jews. In 1990, total per-family philanthropic contributions by Jewish families in America were estimated at $1,600, making Jews comparable to Mormons in per-family dollars contributed.[6]

Levels of giving by individuals vary widely within all denominations. Figure 2 shows three major religious groups–Catholics, mainline Protestants, and conservative Protestants—in which survey respondents from each of the three are divided into five equal parts, called "quintiles." To explain: if we lined up all the Catholics in the United States in a row from the smallest givers to the biggest givers, then counted off and divided them into five groups of equal size, we would have quintiles. Figure 2 shows the amount survey respondents in 1987-1989 reported giving in each of the five quintiles of (1) Catholics, (2) mainline Protestants, and (3) conservative Protestants. The overall pattern is the same in all three groups. The lowest quintile gave nothing, the second averaged only $22 to $26 per family, and the third averaged only $129 to $132 per family. The really big differences occur in the highest quintile. In sum, not only are the amounts given by individuals vastly different within each of the three groups, but the differences *between* the three are almost entirely a matter of what the big givers contribute. Big-giver conservatives far outdistance those in mainline churches and the Catholic church.

The denominations vary widely in their financial practices. On the following pages we will describe them briefly, first the Mormons, then the Assemblies of God, the new megachurches, two mainline denominations (ELCA Lutherans and Presbyterians), the Catholics, and the Jews.

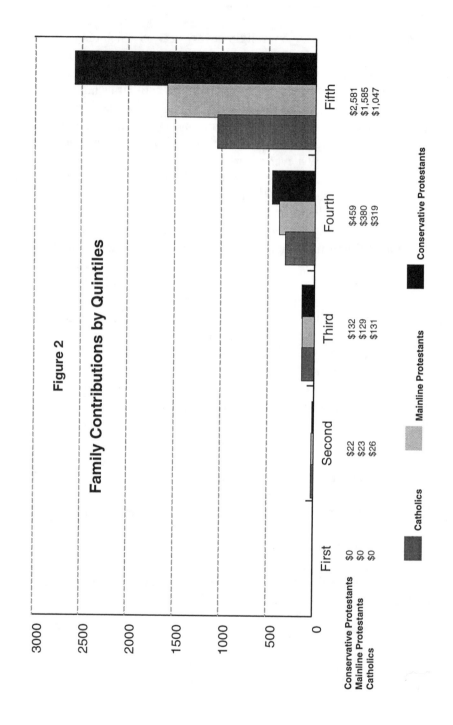

Figure 2

Family Contributions by Quintiles

	First	Second	Third	Fourth	Fifth
Conservative Protestants	$0	$22	$132	$459	$2,581
Mainline Protestants	$0	$23	$129	$380	$1,585
Catholics	$0	$26	$131	$319	$1,047

■ Catholics   ■ Mainline Protestants   ■ Conservative Protestants

The Mormons

The Church of Jesus Christ of Latter-Day Saints (for short, Mormon church) has 4.9 million members in the United States and over 9 million in the world. It is famous for extremely high levels of giving. Annual contributions are roughly 6 percent of the total income of all American Mormons. About 30 to 45 percent pay a full tenth of their pre-tax income.

The Mormon church is unique in a number of ways. It is organized in "wards" that are roughly equivalent to medium-to-large Protestant churches, with 350 to 600 members. If wards become large, they are divided into two, so none grow extremely large. Wards are both worship centers and social centers. Each has an educational program, a youth program (including the Mormon equivalent of Boy Scouts), home teaching through visits to members' homes, and so on. There are no professional clergy in charge. Wards are led by part-time laypersons called "bishops," who serve without pay for terms of three to five years. It is a big job, taking many hours a week, and it rotates among the men in the ward. The annual costs of a ward are very low in comparison with Protestant churches because there are no full-time clergy, no full-time secretaries, and few custodial costs.

Mormons are held responsible for their levels of giving. Once a year each head of household is required to meet with his or her bishop for a "tithing settlement." At this meeting the bishop reviews the person's record of giving. The bishop never asks the household's income, but the two come to an agreement on the person's tithing status—either full tithe payer, partial tithe payer, or nontither. A full tithe payer has paid 10 percent of family income. A nontither is someone who has not contributed anything at all. Husbands and wives have independent tithing status based on their personal income.

All full tithers are given receipts at this meeting and then, if other religious standards of the family's life are in order, they receive a "temple recommend," a one-year document granting access to all Mormon temples. There are forty-three temples around the world, and going to them for ceremonies is important in Mormon religious life. The ceremonies in the temple assure the person of his or her salvation. On the average, Mormons visit temples at least annually, and commonly they do so several times a year. Mormon marriages are often solemnized in temples, and to attend a marriage, everyone—even a family member—needs to have a temple recommend. However, Mormons may, if they desire, marry outside of temples in different kinds of ceremonies.

No one should think that all Mormons tithe or attend church regularly. An average of half of all registered Mormons living in a geographical ward are not regular churchgoers. Over half are not full tithers. Partial tithers and nontithers remain full members of the ward and are welcome at all gatherings. But they are denied some privileges. They are not allowed to enter the temple, and (if youth) they are not allowed to advance up to the levels of priesthood or to go on a two-year mission.

In reality, most ward members do not know which of the other people are tithers and which are not. The bishop never tells. Of course an individual person may tell others, and the word may get around as to who has not been going to the temple. There is usually social pressure in a Mormon ward for a member to become a tither.

Mormon worship services include no talk of money, no appeals, and no offerings. There are no pledges and stewardship campaigns. Members hand their contributions to the ward leaders informally. Mormons tend to think of tithing almost like taxes; it is obligatory, unavoidable, and a normal part of life. Not everyone likes tithing, but it serves as a constant reminder to a Mormon of what is important or unimportant in life and of the need to keep material desires subordinate to spiritual things.

The entire denomination is centralized and computerized. Money collected in each ward is transferred to central headquarters, which in turn gives out grants to each ward to cover annual expenses, based on a formula including number of members, cost of utilities, and so on. No ward is free to stop sending money.

Financial transactions are kept secret. Nobody reports the amounts given by individuals, and denominational leaders make all disbursements without reporting to the laity on how the money is spent. Financial records are not open to individual members.

The Assemblies of God

The Assemblies of God is one of the most vigorous young denominations in America. It was founded in 1914 as a confederation of pentecostal pastors. Its theology is based on the life of the spirit, including speaking in tongues, emotional fervor, and biblical literalism. It teaches discipline and abstinence in life for spiritual purposes—abstinence from drinking, smoking, drugs, nonmarital sex, ostentation, and gambling, though the range of abstinences has decreased over the decades. Whereas the Assemblies of God was at first a church of the poor, today its members are predominantly working class and middle class. In 1994 it reported about 2.3 million members in the United States and over 20 million worldwide.

Pastors in the Assemblies of God have always felt that it should not be allowed to evolve into a denomination like the others; it is still officially called a "movement" or a "cooperative fellowship." Thus the Assemblies of God stresses freedom of pastors to be innovative and entrepreneurial. It avoids any central authority or standardization. Preachers are not required to have seminary training for certification, but they are required to have received the gift of tongues. At all levels—local, district, and national—the pastors clearly have the power. The entire confederation is more an organization of pastors than it is an organization of congregations.

The denominational financial structure is unique in that local ministers (not congregations) are required a pay a tithe to the district office for the annual renewal of their credentials. (The exact meaning of "tithe" varies from district to district, from about 5 percent to 10 percent of total income.) Also unique is the separation of the mission program from denominational budgets. Financial support for missions is not a part of local congregations' budgets; members are asked to make separate pledges to missionaries, and the money is sent directly to Springfield, Missouri world headquarters. Local church councils do not vote on where to send mission money. Money given by individuals to missionaries is funneled through the denominational headquarters, where 5 percent is retained for administrative expenses and another 5 percent goes into an emergency fund. The rest goes to the specified missionaries. In 1994 the total amount given to missionaries was $109 million, while the total amount given to U.S. Assemblies of God congregations was about $1.4 billion.

Unlike most denominations, the Assemblies of God puts little emphasis on membership. Churchgoers are invited to all programs and entitled to all ministries, including marrying and burying, even if they are not members. They are not entitled to be elected to office. In a typical Assembly of God church, less than half of the regular attenders are members. Membership entails the obligations of regular participation, agreement with doctrines, and tithing. Numerous regular attenders are deterred by these requirements and do not become members, even during their entire life. Nobody checks on members to see if they really are tithers or not, and some are clearly not.

Assemblies of God churches have no annual stewardship programs or pledge drives for the congregational budget. The only pledging is for specific missionaries. Sermons on stewardship are not frequent, but sermons on giving one's life to the Lord are constant, and they include mention of tithing and references to Malachi 3:8-10, promising that God will repay tithers with an "overflowing blessing." The high level of giving is not the result of stewardship programs, for such programs do not exist; it is the result of faith in reciprocity with God—that tithing ensures God's eternal blessings and protection.

The New Paradigm Megachurches

In the United States a few churches grew so rapidly and spectacularly in the 1970s and 1980s that they attracted widespread attention. The definition of "new paradigm church" or "megachurch" varies. Scott Thumma, in his doctoral dissertation, uses the criterion of having 2,000 weekly attendance, and by that criterion there were over 350 megachurches in 1990.[7] John Vaughn, a professor at Southwest Baptist University, estimates the number at 400.

Some of the new megachurches are explicitly innovative, others are not. A few of today's megachurches are old inner-city establishment "First Churches," such as First Baptist Church in Dallas or First Methodist in Houston. Most important here are the innovative "new paradigm" megachurches, who clearly see themselves as breaking new ground. Our attention is limited to them. The most famous are Willow Creek Community Church near Chicago (nondenominational), Saddleback Valley Community Church near Los Angeles (Southern Baptist), Community Church of Joy near Phoenix, Arizona (ELCA Lutheran), and Calvary Chapel of Costa Mesa, California (nondenominational).[8]

The new paradigm megachurches tend to be conservative in theology. They are evangelical, fundamentalist, or pentecostal. Their main innovation is in their new methods for reaching unchurched people and their changed conception of evangelism and worship. These churches have devised new ways to attract people turned off to traditional churches, to build relationships with them, and to invite them into a life-changing Christian community. Their members tend to be younger than in other Protestant churches. These churches do not emphasize denominations; the most common denominations are Southern Baptist and Assemblies of God, but about one-half are nondenominational.

Each of these churches tends to have a highly gifted pastor who has built up the membership over the years. The nondenominational mega-churches normally have only a weak governing committee of elected laypersons; the real power remains with the senior pastor and the staff. These churches tend not to operate with annual budgets, but rather to stress tithing and to appeal periodically for special projects and programs.

One innovation is the organizational structure of these churches. They contain a wide variety of specific ministries and groups, almost like a shopping mall of ministries. The physical plants befit this organization. The worship service in the building's auditorium is the overall gathering place, and afterward the people move through mall-like spaces that promote specific groups and ministries, such as religious education classes, spiritual development groups, athletics, theater groups, health clinics, recovery groups, teen activities, music groups, and scout groups.

A second innovation is the use of covenants. Both Saddleback and Willow Creek have two levels of membership, and both require prospective members to sign covenants. At Saddleback, to become a member a person must be baptized and must sign a membership covenant saying that he or she will pray for the church's growth, invite unchurched friends to attend, serve in some ministry of the church, attend faithfully, live a godly life, and give regularly. Anyone declining to do this is not a member, yet is welcome at all church gatherings. Members desiring a higher level of maturity and commitment are invited to attend an annual class called Class 201, in which the ways to spiritual maturity are laid out. At the end, participants are invited to sign a "Growth Covenant" for one year. It stipulates that the person will spend time daily in Bible reading and prayer, give the first 10 percent of his or her income, and fellowship with believers in a small group. This covenant is printed on a membership card good for one year, and if the member wants to continue after that, he or she needs to sign up again later. At present Saddleback has about 5,000 members (called the "Congregation") and about 3,500 who have signed the annual Growth Covenant (called the "Committed"). (Within the committed is another group committed to active ministering to others and leading the church ministries–about 1,500, and they are called the "Core.")[9]

At Willow Creek there is a similar organization of the congregation in concentric circles, with a committed core and an outer penumbra of "seekers." As at Saddleback, the committed group must sign an annual covenant; this was an innovation in recent years.

A third innovation of megachurches is having "seeker services." These are worship services designed specifically for visitors and seekers, not for the committed members. The seeker services are scheduled at the most common church-shopping hour, 11:00 A.M. on Sunday. The seeker services are designed to alleviate the cynicism visitors may have about churches and money; both Saddleback and Willow Creek make announcements at seeker services before the offerings, saying that the offering is solely for the regular attenders and not for visitors. Visitors are welcome guests and are not expected to contribute. Lee Strobel, one of the ministers at Willow Creek, explains that seekers are often highly allergic to talk of money, and the church must recognize that.

> There are no fund-raising thermometers on the walls, no pledge system, no bingo games or car washes, no gimmicks or high-pressure tactics. The Christians support the ministry financially because they have been taught that this is how God underwrites the work of the local church. By exempting visitors from the expectation of giving, the church is sending them a signal that says, "Our agenda is to help you, not to help ourselves."[10]

The level of financial giving in these churches is very high, averaging over $1,000 annually per attender and sometimes much higher. Each has a solid core of enthusiastic members who are tithers and a large outer circle of members who give little or nothing. These churches reject pledging as "too denominational," and they reject annual stewardship programs. Instead, they teach the importance of tithing.

Bill Hybels, pastor of Willow Creek, states that due to the cynicism about church finances today in the unchurched population, all talk about money must be limited to the membership itself. Only with spiritually mature people does he discuss finances. He explains:

> We learned in just the past years . . . that somehow we have to try to bring about a second conversion, and that is to convert a consumer into a contributor.[11]

Hybels teaches that a 10 percent tithe is the foundational amount that a believer should give to the work of the church. He challenges committed members to do their part:

> It's time for more of you to step to the plate who are a part of this church and ask yourself the question, "If everyone else in the church supported this church the way . . . my family supports it, would this church exist?"[12]

Evangelical Lutheran Church in America

The Evangelical Lutheran Church in America (ELCA) has about 3.8 million confirmed members in 11,023 congregations (1995). The average congregation size is 349 adult members. Congregations are governed by elected councils of twelve to twenty-one members who prepare annual budgets and submit them for approval at congregational meetings.

About 70 percent of ELCA congregations have an annual stewardship program, which typically involves sermons, pledges, and promotional material. About 18 percent of the congregations in 1993 reported that they had lay leaders visit every member during the previous year to ask for pledges. According to 1993 research, 56 percent of the congregations use written pledge cards, and 60 percent of laity report that they or someone in their family filled out a pledge card in the previous year. Almost all members use weekly envelopes. Most congregations send members quarterly or annual statements reporting the amount they have given to date. No congregations make public a report of how much each family gives.

Elected parish leaders make decisions about disbursement of funds. Each local congregation is asked to contribute toward denominational mission programs, following a formula that varies from synod to synod. Commonly the amount is from 10 to 20 percent of the expected local offertory. The congregation is not required to pay this amount, though there is pressure to do so, and most pay at least a high proportion of the expected amount. Most congregations also send some financial support to missionaries and service projects outside the denominational mission programs.

The ELCA, like other mainline denominations, is experiencing a decrease in the percentage of the total offering sent on to synods, churchwide organizations, and denominational mission programs. Local churches feel less loyalty and obligation to the denomination than was true several decades ago, and this endangers denominational programs.[13]

Presbyterian Church (U.S.A.)

The Presbyterian Church (U.S.A.) has 2.7 million members and 11,400 congregations (1995). Most of the congregations are small; the average size in 1995 was 235 members. Local congregations are governed by an elected lay council called the "session," composed typically of ten to twenty-five people. The pastor is the moderator and a voting member of the session and presides at all meetings. The session has final authority in most decisions, but not all; decisions about hiring or firing ordained clergy, buying and selling real estate, and taking out large mortgages must be ratified by the congregation and presbytery.

The session is in charge of formulating each annual budget and providing financial support. At an annual meeting all church members are given reports on finances, staff, and plans, but (except in a few special cases) the members cannot overrule the budget set by the session.

About two-thirds of Presbyterian churches hold an annual stewardship drive in the autumn. All large churches do so, but some small ones operate informally. The annual stewardship program involves sermons, appeals by lay leaders, and distribution of promotional material. In 1993, 20 percent of the congregations reported visiting each member during the previous year's stewardship program, and 35 percent reported telephoning some or all of the members. Eighty percent of laity reported that someone in their family had filled out a pledge card in the past year.

Each local church, in order to remain in good standing, must pay an "apportionment" or tax to higher judicatories. The money is split among the presbytery, synod, and national levels. The amount varies from place to place but averaged between $16 and $26 per member in 1995. Other payments to higher judicatories, denominational missions, or special funds are optional. As with the ELCA Lutherans, the Presbyterians are gradually sending a smaller proportion of offerings to denominational missions, instead sending money to other missions and programs. This trend began in the 1960s. In response, denominational offices are working to link congregations with specific mission programs and missionaries the people know personally.

Roman Catholics

The U.S. Roman Catholic Church has 62 million members in 19,700 parishes. Catholic parishes do not have membership lists like Protestant churches, but they have registry lists containing names and addresses of people who voluntarily sign up to receive mailings and envelopes. These lists are rough analogs to Protestant membership lists. Not all Catholics show interest in parish involvement; researchers estimate that about three out of four baptized adult Catholics are on parish registry lists.

Catholic parishes are different from Protestant churches in one important way: size. They average about 2,300 on their registry lists, making them over eight times as large, on average, as Protestant churches. Some are very large. In a 1982 study 16 percent had more than 5,000 registered members.

By canon law the pastor of a parish must be a diocesan priest or religious order priest in good standing. He is financially responsible to the bishop for his parish, and he personally has final authority on all monetary matters. Canon law says that he is required to have a lay parish finance committee, and in addition recent church policy mandates that he must have an elected lay parish council. In the United States today, parish councils are functioning in about three-fourths of the parishes. Some have strong influence on parish life, and others have no influence. In a situation of disagreement or conflict, the parish council has no authority over or against the pastor.

About 40 percent of all Catholic parishes have an elementary school, all of which receive subsidies from parish offerings. The amount of subsidy varies widely. In 1992, in parishes with a school, an average of 30 percent of parish income went to support the school; this percentage is falling each year. The rest of school expenses are covered by tuition and fund raisers.

All parishes are required to pay an assessment to their diocese based on a local formula. Typically it is about 8 to 12 percent of total parish income. Diocesan and national programs, including social service and missions, are supported from this assessment. A series of special offerings are also taken in each parish, averaging eight to twelve a year, commonly with little fanfare. Otherwise pastors and parish leaders, unlike leaders of most Protestant churches, do not decide where to send mission money. The parish pays the assessment to the diocese but sends little money to missions or social programs. An individual member who wants to support specific missions or causes must send the money directly or contribute to the appropriate special offerings during the year.

Catholic giving is below the level of Protestant denominations, as figure 1 showed. Catholic parishes vary greatly on whether or not they have stewardship programs and on how much emphasis they give to them. According to all research, the larger the Catholic parish, the lower is the per-family giving. Envelopes are available in almost all parishes, but use of envelopes is low. About half of American parishes use pledge cards to some extent, though there is little pressure for returning them, and the large majority do not use them. Catholics more than Protestants decide week by week how much they will give. Many Catholics dislike the idea of pledging, and this impedes pastors in their stewardship efforts; in a 1993 survey, only 48 percent of Catholic laity said they approve of the idea of pledging.[14]

Jewish Denominations

The Jewish community is sociologically different from Christian denominations in two important respects. Most important is that its communal organizations are of two types, synagogues and federations. Synagogues are structurally similar to Protestant churches; they typically have 250 to 500 households. About 40 to 45 percent of American Jews are synagogue members. Federations are large committees in each city that coordinate Jewish organizations such as child care centers, social service programs, and youth organizations. Federations are a recent development, about half a century old in the United States, and they have grown up to overcome factional fighting among Jewish organizations. Today they resemble United Way coalitions in each metropolitan area, and they raise and disburse the vast bulk of Jewish charitable giving. The average Jewish family gives more to its federation than to its synagogue. Federations are usually dominated by the established Jewish families in each metropolitan area.

The institutional duality of synagogues and federation results from the double nature of Jewish identity—as a religion and also as a secular ethnic tradition. Many Jews see themselves as unbelievers and secular people, yet at the same time fully Jewish and supportive of federation activities. This situation has no Christian counterpart.

The second unique feature of the Jewish community is that Jews see synagogue giving not as being "charity" but as paying dues to a club. Synagogues sell annual memberships for set fees, just like country clubs. The Christian concepts "stewardship of God's gifts" and "giving to the Lord" have no counterpart in synagogue giving. Most charitable gifts are given directly to the federations.

The American Jewish community is divided into three main branches—Orthodox, Conservative, and Reform. These branches arose in different historical settings. Orthodox Judaism maintains the old European theological and ritual traditions, while Conservative and Reformed Judaism arose in the last two centuries in efforts to embrace parts of European and American culture. The largest branch is Conservative, with about two million members. The Reform have about 1.3 million members, and the Orthodox have about 1 million. There is no central authority in the American Jewish community. Each synagogue is governed by an elected board of directors, with rules varying from locality to locality. Each synagogue owns its own property and makes all its own financial decisions. Rabbis are hired for specific terms of service, usually two years at first, then longer—though practices vary. A rabbi has no recourse if the board of directors of a synagogue decides not to renew an employment contract.

Synagogue dues are set annually by the board of directors. In about two-thirds of the synagogues there is a set fee, typically in the range of $600 to $1200 for a family. Young single people and elderly people are given a lower rate. Usually if a would-be member cannot afford the cost, he or she can talk confidentially with the rabbi or president and ask for a dues abatement. In the other one-third of synagogues there is a "fair share" procedure, in which a prospective member sits down with a committee of the board of directors, states his financial situation and burdens, and comes to a decision with them regarding his fair share. A few synagogues have a scale of dues based on age or income, but this is not very common; most common is a set annual dues figure plus a procedure for giving abatements.

Any Jewish person who does not pay the dues is still welcome at the synagogue, but on the high holy days, when attendance is at its peak and all rooms are crowded, nonpayers cannot get in. Nonpayers are also not entitled to have a child in the Jewish school or to have a synagogue wedding or bar mitzvah. Social pressure commonly builds up against nonpayers, who are made to feel like freeloaders.

In a typical synagogue, two-thirds to three-fourths of the annual budget is raised by dues. The rest is raised in various ways in auctions, art shows, testimonial dinners, and an annual appeal for donations. Giving to synagogues is a private matter, and the amount of dues or gifts paid is never made public. Only in the case of extraordinary gifts (and if the donor agrees) is there recognition given. Of course if a member wants his or her gift to be publicly known, he or she can give it openly at a fund-raising event.

Federation fund raising is more public and more often done through social events, especially celebratory banquets and testimonial dinners. During these banquets pledges are taken, often in a fun-filled competitive spirit. The parties abound in repartee and entertaining one-upmanship, all for a good cause. Usually the amounts pledged are announced publicly. Federation fund drives are major community events, and in every city there is social pressure on affluent Jewish families to make large gifts.

All synagogues owe taxes to the administration of their branch. For example, in the early 1990s conservative synagogues had to pay an annual tax of $30 per member unit, and in addition there was a request for voluntary payment of $20 more to support the seminary. Any synagogue that refuses to pay the annual tax may be disaffiliated from the branch, but this seldom happens. The power at the branch level is clearly with the laity, not the rabbis. Only in the running of seminaries are the rabbis more dominant than the laity.

As noted earlier, total philanthropic giving by Jews is about $1,600 per family. But this money does not go solely to Jewish charities. One researcher estimated that about half goes to non-Jewish causes such as university alumni campaigns, civic groups, and arts groups.[15] It is common for American Jews to give large gifts both to the United Way and also to United Jewish Appeals. The wealthiest families give large gifts, making the Jewish community uncommonly skewed in sizes of gifts— that is, a smaller proportion of families give a higher proportion of the total than is true elsewhere in American society.

Trends in Protestant Stewardship

Future trends in church life depend on spiritual currents, and they are impossible to predict. In past decades when new spiritual energies showed up here or there, established church leaders were taken by surprise. We cannot say much specific about the future. All we can do is make some general statements. Here are four.

First, spiritual needs in America are as strong today as ever, and religious organizations meeting those needs will be as strong in the future as they ever were. The religious market is strong, and the only unknown is who will service that market.

Second, in the future the Protestant giver will want more control over where his or her gift goes and how well it is accounted for. Trust in institutions, either religious or secular, is lower today than at any time since polling began after World War II. The polls also show that the farther an institution is away from the individual, the faster the drop in trust.[16] We may expect more giving to designated causes, less giving to denominational bodies in general. This trend has affected national denominations and their programs, making older financial arrangements unworkable for the future. The future will see more pressure to relax central denominational controls and to remodel denominations in the direction of looser networks of churches.[17]

Third, all observers agree that baby boomers and post baby boomers feel less denominational loyalty than their parents did. Why, they ask, should we pay for something that isn't important? The element of denominational life most financially vulnerable is centralized authority, certification, and standardization.

Fourth, probably the greatest overall trend is the new emphasis on stewardship of wealth accumulated over the years by church members. This emphasis gives new attention to planned giving, wills, annuities, and endowments. This trend is being driven by the accumulation of trillions of dollars of wealth among American church members and the willingness of these people to give large gifts to their churches for the future. In 1990 *Fortune* magazine estimated that an unprecedented $7 trillion has now been accumulated by Americans 60 or older. We return to this topic in chapter 7.

For Reflection and Discussion

1. Why do you think the level of financial giving tends to be high in Assemblies of God, Mormon, and megachurches? What practices of these groups might benefit your congregation? How could these be implemented?

2. Why do Jewish synagogues see paying annual dues as a normal and obvious practice, while Christian churches oppose the idea?

3. Who has final authority for setting the budget and managing finances in your congregation? How do the pastor and board proceed when they disagree about financial matters? Is the procedure respectful and productive? If not, how could it be changed?

4. Does your congregation conduct "fund raisers" (one-time or annual events offering a product or service in return for a donation or payment)? Why or why not? How do you view fund raising in light of your understanding of "stewardship"?

5. To what degree do you think members of your congregation view their pledge or donations as "dues"? In what circumstances, if any, are donations made public in your congregation? Does your denomination specify the level of support expected from your congregation? Which, if any, of these practices would you change if you could? Why?

CHAPTER 3

Why Give Money to the Church?

We need to ask an elementary question: Why give money to the church at all? For that matter, why give monetary gifts to anyone? Anthropologists and economists have looked at gift-giving behavior from all angles. In this chapter we will explicate some of their conclusions. Our discussion is based on the disciplines of economics and sociology, not theology, but we think it has insights and lessons for everyone.

Let us state a beginning axiom in this field: From a purely individual economic point of view, monetary gifts of any kind make no sense. Why give money away when it would be useful for something else a person really wants? How is giving money away different from throwing it into the sea?

Economists have discussed this question since the path-breaking theoretical work by Kenneth Boulding.[1] This line of analysis comes to an important conclusion: Most voluntary gift giving is not really gift giving at all. The money is given in order to *obtain* something the giver wants. Put differently, a gift giver is usually hoping to buy something. A businessman giving a thousand dollars to the local hospital, or to the opera company, or even to the church is doing it in hopes of buying something. He may want to buy good feelings in the community, ties to important people, blessings for himself and his family, or even self-affirmation. We believe this theoretical starting point is correct, so long as a few possible limitations and misconceptions are clarified. (We will discuss them below.) A second axiom can now be stated: gift-giving to the church as well as to anyone else is rational behavior, done with a definite end in mind.

We need to be clear about the word *rational*. Economic theorists begin with the "rational actor" model, assuming that a person resembles a chess player, dispassionately thinking through all the ramifications of his or her moves. This model is useful for some purposes but ultimately misleading in real life because it is blind to a large portion of human behavior. Humans have psychological drives: they fall in love, they live in families, they build up feelings about other people, and they engage in endless rituals incomprehensible to the economic theorist.

In our analysis here, we understand rational behavior to include considerations of feelings and personal relationships. This behavior takes the long view about one's life, not just a calculation about profit or loss today. There are times when a touching personal experience, a moving sermon, or the wishes of a loved one influence one's behavior, making it depart from the chess player ideal.

We need to be able to see the world through the eyes of the people making the decisions. Consider an anthropologist studying a native tribe. He or she may be baffled as to why the natives carry out religious dances season after season. The anthropologist may give up trying to understand and conclude that the natives are irrational. But this only tells us that the anthropologist is a failure. The dances *are* rational from the world view of the natives, within their own social setting and in the context of their own sentiments and passions, whatever the assessment of outsiders. The same is true of religious behavior. No one should expect it to be fully understood by outsiders.

Motives for Giving

We need to say a word or two about motives. Human motivation is one of the most difficult topics in psychological research. Motivation is complex, multilayered, and partly hidden from the actor's own con-sciousness. It cannot be assessed by asking anyone "Why did you decide to do that?" because the response will unavoidably be filtered and sani-tized, even if the respondent is trying to be completely honest. Research into motivation needs to be done indirectly through use of projective instruments, actual test situations, and inferences from real behavior. Human motives are always mixed and obscure, even to the actor. We agree with the Danish philosopher Soren Kierkegaard who said that "Purity of heart is to will one thing," but actual human nature does not allow this. As we study actual human behavior, we need to accept the reality of mixed, not-always-noble, human motives.

Anyone trying to study motivation is thus left with making inferences and guesses. Numerous psychologists and economists have made lists of motivations for gift-giving, but there is no way to declare that one is more accurate than the other.[2] We see no way to escape this problem.

Four Main Motives for Church Giving

Our research has depicted four main motives for financial gifts to churches. We cannot prove this conclusion compellingly and with scientific precision, but we are certain we have identified the main motives. They are (1) reciprocity with a social group, (2) reciprocity with God, (3) giving to extensions of the self, and (4) thankfulness. Readers may ask why altruism is not in this list. The reason is that altruism should not be seen as a separate motivation. It is present to some degree in and alongside the other motives, and it is best understood as an element of others, not standing by itself. We explain below.

Reciprocity with a Social Group

To explain reciprocity with a social group we need to take a look at secular fund raising. Most of the social science research on gift giving has been done on secular, not religious, philanthropy. Several excellent research studies have been done, usually based on interviews with philanthropic givers.[3] They all agree that philanthropy (especially among big givers) is a product of social relationships between donors, their peers, and recipient organizations. People make philanthropic gifts as one act in an ongoing chain of acts intended to strengthen social ties and to gain esteem from other people. This is especially true of wealthy people, who have excess money to spend and are often ready to use it to buy recognition and esteem from peers. Involvement in nonprofit organizations and contributions to these organizations are one way of gaining recognition.

Professional fund raisers know how the system works. Large gifts for any cause can be obtained only through personal requests, made by highly esteemed people who are already friends with the prospective donor. This is expressed in the common slogan, "Individuals give to individuals." It is true. Teresa Odendahl interviewed philanthropic givers and cited how they commonly thought about these matters. One donor:

> The person who asks you to give can be significant. Certain people, in my view, have great influence. If one of those asks someone else of that caliber, it becomes important for the other person to respond—in part because next month I will have something cooking. It's, if you scratch my back I'll scratch your back, type of thing.[4]

In order to raise funds from their peers, local social leaders must themselves first make sizable contributions and must mention this when talking with their friends. The most valuable caller in a fund-raising campaign is a beloved and respected local celebrity, a person who many others in the community want to think well of them. Every town and city has some of these people. When they ask someone for a gift they in effect offer a relationship of reciprocity with the prospect, and if the prospect makes a gift, a positive bond is built. Normally the caller phones or writes a note of thanks. The new donor thus activates an obligation from the caller to reciprocate in some way later. A year or so later the donor can call on the same friend and say, "Joe, I was happy I could help you last year. Can I come and talk to you about an important project in this community that a group of us are working on?"

Odendahl found that most gift givers want their gift to be well known. She estimated that over 80 percent did. Fund raisers know that the best method is to have leading citizens make personal calls. Ideally the campaign begins at the top of the social pyramid in the community and works down, so that the highest-status person calls on five or ten other people on the first or second tier of status, and they do the same, working down.

We are describing this system because it is a pure example of human reciprocity. When individuals interact with each other, for example in doing favors for each other, a bond of reciprocity develops. The relationship includes an understanding on the part of both people that they can call on each other for help and can trust each other. Reciprocal relationships are precious for the people in them, for they are win-win deals. They provide the gratifications of friendship plus the assurance that the other person can be called on if needed. Reciprocal relationships grow slowly because a time of testing is required, and strong reciprocal relationships take time. They also carry a cost because the person who does a favor is entitled to come calling later and to ask for a favor in return; when this is done the only possible answer is yes. But after saying yes the donor can call on his friend again later.

Odendahl raises the question of why donors give, let us say, $10,000 to each other's favorite nonprofit, when they could simply give $10,000 to their own favorite cause without bothering anyone else. The financial result would be the same. But this is seldom done, and Odendahl explains that the relationship of reciprocity has value in itself, quite apart from the money. The benefits of these reciprocal ties are so great that people try hard to keep the ties strong. Contributing to each other's philanthropic projects is a good way.

Secular fund raisers know that people prefer local causes over national ones because personal relationships are primarily local. Successful fund raising is usually for causes on which local people of means agree; it cannot be successful for anything that implies social criticism or a lack of appreciation of the local notables. The safest causes are education, culture, the arts, and health organizations such as hospitals.

We need to explain that the dynamics of reciprocity may carry a cost because some requests for assistance may be turned down by Person X, and the word will get around. Then people will whisper about Person X, who everyone knows has the money and seems to want to be known as someone who carries his or her own weight, but who, can you believe it, refused to make a pledge to this year's campaign!

Several conditions are required for this social reciprocity to stimulate fund raising. The caller and the prospect need to know each other— the closer the relationship, the better. The caller must assure the donor that he and others in the social network will know of the gift's size and will appreciate the gift. The caller should represent, if possible, a larger social circle, all of whom would be favorably impressed by a sizable gift to the cause. It is a transaction: money spent to buy human bonds and esteem.

We are talking about human reciprocity because this explains the majority of secular philanthropy in America. Most gifts—and without a doubt most large gifts—are given as part of a larger agenda of strengthening reciprocal relationships seen as valuable for the future.

Numerous times we have been told by pastors that the motive of reciprocity with a social group applies more to wealthy people than to others. We have no compelling evidence to test this statement, but we are inclined to believe it. Several pastors have told us that affluent people think more about social recognition for their gifts than do the nonaffluent. Possibly it is true that affluent people in general are more attuned to personal esteem and social status in their behavior than others.

How about church giving? Without a doubt the dynamics of reciprocity with a social group exist when churches raise funds or ask for pledges. For churches as for secular organizations, the largest gifts are gotten when esteemed leaders of the church personally visit others. For churches as for secular organizations, most people visualize the reactions of their friends and fellow members when they ponder whether and how much to give. The key question is: Who will see this pledge card? How public will be the knowledge about the size of this gift?

The issue facing churches is not whether reciprocity with a social group is a motive in giving. It is. The issue is a theological one: should reciprocal relationships in the congregation be emphasized or de-emphasized in fund-raising campaigns? It comes down to practical questions: Who will see the pledge cards? Will the size of the pledges be widely known? If the campaign is for a new church building or addition, will there be rooms named after big givers or plaques on the pews or windows displaying who paid for them? We return to these questions in chapter 4.

Reciprocity with God

Whereas reciprocity with a social group is basic to all forms of fund raising, another kind of reciprocity is unique to religious fund raising and religious people. It is reciprocity with God.

As we said earlier, in a relationship of reciprocity a favor from Person X given to Person Y induces an obligation that Person Y will return the favor later. What if Person Y is very powerful, for example, a U.S. senator? Then the relationship takes on more importance. Then thousands of people will wish to build up a reciprocal relationship with him or her. Individuals and organizations will stand in line to make "gifts" to the senator. The reason is simple: senators (especially if they are on key senate committees) can influence appropriations and regulations controlling billions of dollars. Few business leaders, if approached by a representative of the Senate or of, let us say, the Republican National Committee, can refuse to make a gift to the senator or the party. Millions of dollars in "gifts" (actually payments) flow each year into the political party treasuries. For a person to give such a gift is a rational act, done in hopes of gaining something important later.

These political "gifts" are given only under certain conditions. The giver must be certain that the senator will know of the gift and is open to building up a relationship of reciprocity. The giver must also have faith that the senator will try to reciprocate later. That is, the donor needs to know that the senator is open to making a deal. The giver must also believe that the senator will have enough power to make a difference in the future. If any of these conditions are absent, giving the gift is pointless.

With this example we can understand reciprocity with God. God is eternal and omnipotent. God can bestow gifts far greater than any politician. Anyone who believes that God is open to reciprocal relationships will not hesitate for an instant to make immense gifts. If a representative of God came calling, no one would refuse to make a sacrificial gift of great price.

We recently saw a cartoon of a well-dressed businessman in church, with eyes closed and on his knees in prayer, saying quietly to God, "Now here's the deal."

It depends on belief and faith. Is God really open to building up reciprocal relationships? Is God mindful of gifts from individuals, and will God make an effort to repay them later? In short, does God reward big givers? Maybe God is such an impersonal force or being that the whole idea of personal reciprocity with God is wrong from the beginning. It depends on the world view of the donor.

What should ministers and priests say to these questions? What does the tradition say? What is the truth? We will treat this topic in more detail in chapter 4, but we need to make a few observations here.

Reciprocity with God is a powerful motivation for some Christian people, but it has risks. The Book of Job is the *locus classicus* for the theological problem that arises. What if a believer accepts a deal and does his or her part, but the payoffs never come? Job was in distress because he thought he was doing everything right. He believed in reciprocity with God and lived a righteous and generous life in good faith, but the rewards never came. On the contrary, his life got worse and worse. He was tempted to give up his faith and declare that God either did not exist or did not show any interest in him. Faith in reciprocity with God, that is, is dangerously subject to disproof in real life. Social theorist Max Weber said that this is the weakest and most vulnerable part of Christian doctrine in modern times.[5]

Preachers can act as God's agents, analogous to officers of the Republican National Committee coming to call. They can ask for a gift and promise that God will repay it many times over in the future. Preachers can act as stockbrokers, promoting investment opportunities that are certain to pay off well. Preachers can also act as insurance salesmen, recommending policies that are of manageable cost now and that will take care of any future needs, no matter how great. Or preachers can refuse to act in any of these capacities if they do not believe in reciprocity with God.

These questions are not idle ones. As is the case with stockbrokers and insurance agents, the preacher is not a disinterested bystander. Quite the contrary: he or she is intensely interested because his or her job and salary are at stake. Church members know this, and it gives rise to skepticism and even cynicism. Pastors know it also, and some feel compromised.

Giving to Extensions of the Self

Above we said that from an economic rationality point of view, giving money away is irrational because then the actor has less left for himself or herself. This is true. But we need to know who "himself" or "herself" refers to. It may sound simple, but in reality it is not.

What is included in the self? Let us illustrate. Suppose one of us gives a thousand dollars to our spouse. Is this a philanthropic gift? It does not *feel* like it. Is it an occasion of joy or of bitterness? For those of us who are in love, giving the gift produces joy. It does not feel like a loss of a thousand dollars—because we are really giving the gift to ourselves.

Suppose one of us gives a thousand dollars to our grown son or daughter. Is this a philanthropic gift? Does it produce joy or bitterness? It all depends on what we feel about that person. Put simply, it depends on love. Love causes the self to be extended. A loving person includes numerous other people in his or her self, psychologically speaking. A miser does not. A loving person has, as we say, "a big heart" and, in our terms, an encompassing self.

The point here is simply that the self is not clearly bounded. How do we know its limits? Psychologist William James gave us a clue. He said that any person or thing is included in the self if, when we hear that other person or thing praised or criticized, we feel a wave of joy or pain. It all depends on feelings. If a person feels pain when his hometown is ridiculed, that hometown is included in his self. If a person feels pain when her college alma mater is defeated or criticized in some way, that college is included in her self.

Extensions of the self most typically involve a spouse and family members—at least. The needs and desires of these other people are typically so important that they are felt to be little different from the actor's own needs. To illustrate this motivation for giving, let us take an example from donation of living organs.

Example: A Study of Kidney Donors

A research study was recently done on kidney donors. Roberta Simmons of the University of Pittsburgh looked at people who would be willing to donate a kidney if a member of the family needed a kidney to survive. We need to explain here that humans can survive well on one healthy kidney, so donating a kidney is not life-threatening, though it is painful and leaves a large scar. When physicians asked family members about possibly donating kidneys, 86 percent of the sick persons' mothers and fathers, 66 percent of their children, and 47 percent of their siblings soon volunteered. Apparently fathers and mothers most commonly include the sick person in their selves. The majority of kidney donors, when asked, decided instantaneously to give. Their response was immediate: "Of course I will donate."

Simmons explains: "Their decision seems driven by a norm to help a family member in severe difficulty." After donating kidneys the donors were interviewed twice, once shortly after the operation and later

after five to nine years had elapsed. Most donors felt positive about the
experience, and they showed higher self-esteem than nondonors (that is,
than other family members who did not donate a kidney). The operation
was painful, but the result of the whole experience was joyful for all.[6]

It is worth noting that the doctors seeking donors did not think to
look beyond the family. Probably they would have found rapidly de-
creasing percentages agreeing to donate if they asked (a) spouses, (b)
more distant blood relatives, (c) longtime work partners, or (d) longtime
fellow church members. (We have no information on the rank ordering
of these four. Would, for example, spouses donate a kidney more readily
than a more distant blood relative? We can only speculate.) Our point
in recounting the story here is that the self includes other people—especially family members—and that gifts to extensions of the self are not
felt to be losses at all. They produce joy, love, and spiritual growth.
They are rational acts, and they account for billions of dollars each year
in donations.

Some church members feel as if their church is a family, and they
include it in their extended self. They will feel joy when they give gifts
to the church, even without any thoughts about reciprocity. They will
feel joy when they give gifts to their beloved college alma mater.

Extensions of the self are not permanent. We love some people
more one year than the next year. We love our church more one year
than the next, and the same is true of our college alma mater and our
local political leaders. From this analysis we see the importance of having church leadership that is able to nurture feelings of love and belong-
ing among the members.

Thankfulness

Pastors have told us that church members sometimes make gifts out of a
feeling of gratitude. They tell of religious people—although possibly not
a majority—who develop a sense of gratitude for the many gifts God has
given them, and they make gifts to churches and missions as a response.
It is a little like giving in a relationship of reciprocity, except without
any real expectation of future repayment. We would expect this motive
to occur mostly when an earnest Christian believer experiences a special
blessing. People might feel the desire to make gifts to God after re-

covery from an illness, at completion of a successful journey, or at the baptism of a grandchild. A natural human response at such a time would be to feel thankful to God and to make a thank offering. Pastors have told us that some parishioners give out of thankfulness, and it is part of a person's spiritual development to learn to discern the many blessings one has received from God.

How about the rest of life, not just occasions of good fortune like the completion of a trip? Are we humans not receiving gifts continually from God? The answer is a matter of perception, and it depends on one's theological views. Stewardship theology commonly stresses that we are always receiving gifts, and it encourages giving gifts in thankfulness. This motive can be observed, for instance, in an appeal for gifts to poor Christians in third world nations or for hapless victims of an earthquake or typhoon: "You are fortunate, through no merit of your own, while these people are suffering terribly from the earthquake, also through no fault of their own." A motive for responding to such an appeal might be thankfulness that we are not in such dire straits, as well as a tinge of guilt that we have unmerited good fortune in life.

The motive of giving to the church out of gratitude undoubtedly exists, but we are unclear if it is a major motive for giving, operating over long periods of time. Proponents of a stewardship approach told us that this motive can become salient in church members' lives. We heard pastors in mainline churches preach about giving out of gratitude. Those pastors strove to sharpen people's vision of the gifts God has given them because this vision is important in spiritual growth and it strengthens a person's desire to return time, talent, and treasure in gratitude.

We are unable to assess how important a motive thankfulness is. The strength of the thankfulness motive is partly dependent on a theological vision of the gifts one is receiving from God, so we would expect it to be more prominent among theologically committed people than those weak in faith.

Paying for Services Rendered

We need to add a word about a motive noted by other researchers. It is a feeling by the giver that he or she needs to "pay my dues," "pay my fair share," or "pay for services rendered." This feeling clearly exists. It arises from a realization that churches cost money to run, and that everyone is morally obligated to chip in. In many social organizations or events in life there are dues or payments of a fair share. Often the amount is stated openly, and people come to expect it. But in Christian churches the amount is never stated openly, and herein lies a complication. As we said, Jewish synagogues are different in that they have an annual membership fee like a country club or swimming club. Members pay the annual fee willingly, so long as it seems reasonable and fair, because everyone knows that there are real costs.

In Christian churches the concepts of "dues" and "fair share" are seldom discussed. The amount of money a member owes is never stated openly. It is like being a member of a country club without set dues but with a moral obligation to contribute. What should the person pay? How much is expected? The member is forced to make his or her own calculation, and one possible method is to divide the annual budget by the number of family units.

But what is the *motivation* to pay? Why pay one's fair share if you do not have to? In a Protestant church nobody checks up, and on top of that, nobody really knows what the "fair share" is. In this situation it is rational behavior to pay less than one's fair share with the hope that others will step forth and pay more to keep the organization going. This is called "free riding" by economists, and the expression comes from the practice of riding free on city buses if no one checked whether passengers had bought tickets. Why not ride free, avoid detection, and save money? It becomes a moral, subjective issue. Free riding is widespread in various sectors of society. Examples are listening to public radio and taking advantage of social agencies supported by the United Way. The general public can enjoy these commodities without being forced to pay at all.

We need to be clear that if a motive for giving is reciprocity with God, there is no free riding. No one can avoid detection because God sees all. But if reciprocity with God as a motive is absent, the temptation to ride free is real and is indeed empirically common. It pays off for the individual, but it hurts the organization. Free riding can be suppressed by a system in which everyone knows that church leaders or pastors monitor the giving by individuals. If they know the giving by all the members (not just the pledges), free riding is impossible. In small communities and small churches it is widely assumed that the leadership group knows the level of giving of all members, and thus free riding is infrequent.

Free riding has been offered by some researchers as a major explanation for denominational differences in church giving. The theory states that giving is higher in evangelical denominations because they have a stronger motive of reciprocity with God and they have more obligatory visible indicators of commitment. If a church has rules that disallow lukewarm members from continuing in good standing, those rules will cut down on financial free riding. In addition, having small churches in which people know each other and in which lay leaders monitor the giving by individuals will constrain free riding. We believe these theories are correct.

One of our main points here concerns the concept of "paying my dues" or "paying my share." This should not be seen as a distinct motivation for giving. It is merely a method for determining *how much* to give. The motivation behind it turns out to be the same as in other giving.

Appeals to the Four Motivations

Let us exemplify what the four appeals sound like in action. First, appeals for giving based on reciprocity with the social group might sound like, "Make a pledge and we will include you in the list of donors for the project." Or, "Everyone in this church needs to do his or her part to keep it going."

A lay leader making personal calls might say it like this: "Joe, you and I have known each other in this town a long time. I know that you care about the place. I think this campaign is important to all of us, and I have already made a pledge of X dollars. I would appreciate your considering making a pledge too. Can you look over this material and get back to me?"

A sermon stressing reciprocity with God would go like this: "Give your tithe to God, and God will take care of your needs now and in eternity." Or, "Anyone who gives God a tithe will never have to worry about finances." Or, "Give to God, and God will repay you." Or, "Sow generously, and you will reap generously." Television evangelists often make this sort of appeal in a way mainline Protestants find theologically objectionable.

An appeal based on giving to extensions of the self might sound like this: "This church has been important to this town and to your family. I know it has been important in your life. Help us keep it healthy for our families in the years to come." Or, "Help us make this church something your family will be proud of."

An appeal based on thankfulness: "God has blessed you mightily. You can thank God by helping some of God's less fortunate children." Or, "Do something worthwhile with your money. You can't take it with you." Or, "You have been fortunate in life. God has blessed you richly, and you can return a portion to God in thanks."

Are There Other Appeals?

We believe the four motives described above are the main ones behind substantial gifts to churches. No doubt there are others that exist for some individuals, but not as strong as these. For example, one person told us of the idea of a loan from God as a motivation; the believer with this motive gives money to God as a payback for an earlier loan of good gifts in life. Another person described self-sacrifice as a spiritual motivation in giving, seeing sacrifice as spiritually nourishing, similar to fasting. No doubt these motivations exist, but we doubt that they are foremost.

Let us look at the common themes of stewardship theology. Do they motivate? What about the biblical teaching that we are merely stewards of God's gifts, not owners of them, and that we are accountable to God for what we do with it all? Stewardship sermons include various of the motivations we described. Commonly they begin with Jesus' parables about stewards (or in today's terms, managers) of estates for their owners. Some sermons stress our accountability to the owner, who sooner or later will return and will demand an accounting. In these sermons, the master, upon returning, will say about our stewardship either "Well done, thou good and faithful servant," or "Depart from me." These are instances of reciprocity with God.

Other sermons stress that we do not own anything in the world but merely use the good things in our lives for a while, after which they will pass to someone else to use. These sermons stress our responsibility to take care of our homes, churches, schools—and even our environment, for the sake of future generations. This might be called reciprocity with history. It is most common when the teachings turn to stewardship of creation, as in environmental and ecological care of the planet and of living things. We do it out of a sense of obligation to God and to future generations, hoping that someday they will call us blessed.

Other appeals are often made in American churches. One is guilt: "You people ought to be supporting this church and its ministry better than you are." Another is obligation: "Members of this church are obligated to carry their weight in supporting (this budget or this project)." Both of these appeals are negative rather than positive, thus limited in power and even likely to cause psychological damage to the church community. Negative motivators are never enduring; all motivational research agrees on this.[7]

The Role of Faith

Let us be clear about the role of faith in the four motives. All four depend on faith of some kind, either faith in God or faith in social peers. In secular fund raising, no one will make large gifts to any organization or cause if he or she does not have faith in the honesty, reliability, and integrity of the group in charge. The motive of reciprocity with God depends on faith in God, not just in local leaders.

A practical problem in mainline churches is that nobody can assume that all the members are people of strong faith in God. The mainline churches today have members with all varieties and intensities of faith in God, including no faith at all. Thus many people's motivations do not include reciprocity with God; their motivations are the same as motivations for giving to secular organizations.

A 1990 interview study of adults who grew up in Presbyterian churches and now were in their thirties or forties found that about half of the people were what the researchers called "lay liberals."[8] That is, they took religion seriously and especially its moral code and community life, but they did not believe that their denomination, or even Protestantism in general, had exclusive truth about God and humanity. The lay liberals were universalistic when it came to basic religious authority, and they were tolerant of various religious teachings and traditions—even non-Christian traditions. They could not make themselves criticize the other religions, and had no desire to send out missionaries to convert members of other religions to Christianity. Rather, they believed that most religions are somehow valid. Lay liberals have evolved a different sort of faith than traditional evangelical Protestantism. Their specific denominational identities were very weak, their faith in the received traditions was moderately weak, and their commitment to their specific churches was moderately strong. Lay liberals cannot be expected to respond well to appeals based on strong faith in the specific teachings of the Old or New Testament. They are little different from secular people in the way they think about monetary gifts.

In every Protestant church there are some practical hard-nosed types who will hear stewardship theology as only high-sounding pious phrases and a distraction from good "straight talk" about the church's budget and plans. They will say under their breath, "Just cut the blah-blah about stewardship and tell me about next year's budget and what my fair share is." Church leaders need to craft appeals to both faithful and faithless, for both kinds of parishioners are found in the churches. Both are willing to make contributions, each for their own reasons, to support the church.

We became acquainted with mainline Protestant pastors who were confused and frustrated about stewardship. One of the sources of frustration is pertinent to our discussion here. It is the difficulty of teaching a theology of stewardship that really connects with parishioners. Mainline Protestant churches have many members who live in a mixture of theological and secular world views. Such people intuitively understand secular fund-raising appeals because secular fund-raising methods have been developed to speak to the broad semi-secular culture of middle-class Protestantism. These people can understand budgets, projections, visions, percentage giving, pledging, and how to run pledge campaigns. But they do not always grasp the biblical motivations for stewardship of time, talent, and treasure in their lives. They are not motivated by promises of reciprocity with God. In short, they see church giving through the eyes of secular fund raising. Raising funds for the church is seen as one more example of raising funds for the hospital, for the college, and for the community chest. Several pastors told us they could not seem to move many parishioners beyond this way of thinking, so they (the pastors) might as well be doing secular fund raising.

Pastors need to assess what kind of appeal really speaks to the parishioners. Parishioners vary, and they are not always forthcoming about their ultimate motivations for giving. Some will respond to teaching that God will repay all of their gifts. Others will not believe in reciprocity with God and will be motivated only by reciprocity with the social group, by giving to the extended self, or by feelings of thankfulness. Still others will turn a deaf ear to all appeals and will give only a small amount to allow them to feel that they are doing their part to pay the bills.

Once we understand the four motivations, we can understand some of the conundrums of church finances. This is the topic of chapter 4.

For Reflection and Discussion

1. Which motivation inspires the most members of your congregation? To what degree do you think you or another pastor has influenced members in this regard?

2. How do you think God responds to our gifts? What evidence supports your view? What evidence do you see to the contrary?

3. Review the methods used for your congregation's last several stewardship appeals. What was the primary motivation for giving underlying each appeal? How effective was each appeal? What role do you think the motivation played in the effectiveness of the appeal?

4. What other types of motivation can you identify? How important do you think each of these is to members of your congregation?

CHAPTER 4

The Four Motivations in Church Life

We have stated the four main motivations that propel church giving. Related to each are practical issues.

Issues Related to Reciprocity with the Social Group

Reciprocity with the social group is a clear motivation for some people to give. This is not at issue; everyone agrees. At issue is whether to encourage it, discourage it, or direct it in some way or other. In practice this becomes largely a matter of who knows about gifts. We will discuss the question under two headings: (1) Who should look at the pledges? and (2) Should large gifts be publicly recognized?

Who Should Look at the Pledges?

Many pastors we talked with said that neither they nor the finance committee look at pledges—as a matter of principle. Their reason is that looking at pledges violates Christian teachings about human equality before God; pastors and leaders should treat all members equally, and knowing the size of members' gifts makes that impossible. Some ministers told us that in the past when they looked at pledges, it poisoned relationships with some wealthy parishioners who gave only peanuts, while causing them to have deferential attitudes to others who made impressive gifts. A few told us that it made them angry when they saw how little some of the well-off families were giving. The majority reported that their seminary professors advised them never to look at pledges.

These pastors acknowledged that it is tempting for pastors to look at the pledges because of the greater power and confidence it would give them in congregational affairs, yet they resist doing it. The following conversations illustrate various perspectives on this question:

A veteran Presbyterian pastor:

PASTOR: Being human, we pastors all have the tendency—and I'm one of the greatest sinners—if not consciously then subconsciously to get over to the hospital quicker for the big giver than for the little giver. So I don't trust myself that much.

INTERVIEWER: What would you suggest if you were making policy for the whole denomination?

PASTOR: Pastors should not look. Pastors are sinners! And I think the tendency would be, no matter how much you deny it on the surface, that if one-dollar-a-year giver Peggy were in the hospital, you might wait three days, whereas if three-thousand-dollar-a-year Jane were in, you might pole-vault over to the hospital. I think that's within our capacity. And I just don't like it! I don't trust myself enough, or other pastors. In our church even the session and stewardship committee don't know. When we send our pledge canvassers out, some people have asked if there is any possibility of at least putting last year's giving on that card so we know where we're going. And the answer from me is no. No. No. No.

INTERVIEWER: What if a pastor said, "I know how much the people give, and I treat them all the same."

PASTOR: I'd say, "Boy, you are a real saint! You've got more skills than I. And while consciously you might say you do, I'll bet subconsciously if push came to shove, you would make some kind of a discrimination between the heavy and the not so heavy."

INTERVIEWER: What is the empirical reality, if you had to guess, in the Presbyterian denomination? Does the average pastor look, or not?

PASTOR: I would guess that the average pastor would tell you that he doesn't, but probably he does.

INTERVIEWER: Maybe some people would argue that if the pastor doesn't know, then some people will say, "To heck with giving. I'll just toss in a penny." That could happen.

PASTOR: Well, I'm sure it does happen.

In this pastor's church only the bookkeeper and the chair of the steward-ship committee know the size of pledges. The pastor has an understand-ing with the stewardship committee chair:

PASTOR: If from his knowledge of the people who gave, the committee chair felt that there were some who he felt were grossly undergiving, and some who had a lot of money and were giving tremendously, he should let me know. Now, I used that information in two ways. The under-givers I tried to involve in the life of the church because I felt that involvement in the church would enhance their concern for its life and missions. And on the other end, when I know that a certain individual is in a position to give and give well, to that person I would go, and have gone, when I have a specific project. But that person got no better or worse pastoral care than anyone else.

Other pastors made the opposite argument. They said it was essen-tial for their pastoral effectiveness to know everyone's giving record. A pastor of a large Presbyterian church:

I have heard people in seminaries give the advice to pastors: "Never look at what the people give because if you know what they give, that will affect your feeling toward them." My answer to that is, "Well, it sure should!" I know what the people in *this* church give. Not to the dollar, but roughly. And the session knows that I know. I don't believe the other members know. I go through the lists. For instance, when we were looking for a special kind of person to lead one of our things, I said, "Let me see the list of the top 10 percent of givers," and I went through it.

Another Presbyterian pastor gave us his views about who should look at the pledges.

PASTOR: The pastor and stewardship committee should look at the pledges, and the people should know it. I know that the danger is that some pastors aren't management-type people, and some personalities might use that information in a way that's inappropriate. But fund rais-ers need to know what people are giving! A pastor is a fund raiser. A president of a college is a fund raiser. The head of any nonprofit institu-tion is a fund raiser, a person who has to generate gifts from individuals and make grants. In this church I look at the pledges, and the people here know it.

We produce a spread sheet of everybody's pledges this year tabled by his or her pledge last year, and ask the computer if anybody is very far behind. We'll send letters out to those people. The stewardship committee and I review the spread sheet and we target givers. How can you target givers if you don't know? I make house calls on individuals and discuss their pledge. How could I do that if I didn't know their pledge? How could I know, for example, that there are two individuals who really cut their pledges significantly—and the trustees want me to visit those persons and ask if everything is okay. I'm not going to do it deceitfully, and go there and pretend to the person that I don't know about the pledge, and just say "How are you doing?" over and over, and just keep fishing for information to see if maybe they just bought a new cottage or something, and maybe that's why they cut their pledge. So now I can just go and sit down with them and say, "Your pledge is a substantial reduction. Are you upset?" I've got one guy in the church who cut his pledge because I preached a sermon in favor of homosexuals. He cut his pledge. Well, he now knows that all the elders and all the trustees know he cut that pledge.

INTERVIEWER: So there's no hiding.

PASTOR: No, there's no hiding. If you cut your pledge, there are consequences. . . . And there's another thing about knowing the pledges. In churches where the pledges are kept sacrosanct they will have individuals who rise to leadership in the church and become officers in the church and not be pledging or supporting the church. In our church you don't get to be on the session or a deacon or trustee unless you're a pledger.

INTERVIEWER: What if someone advocated that no Presbyterian preacher should ever look at the pledges—just to be certain?

PASTOR: I would say that there's *no way* that a minister is not going to know who is making the big gifts to the church, even if you don't look at the pledges. Everybody tells you who the big givers are. You're not in the church three weeks before people are saying, "By the way, Mr. Smith does such and such." It's not the exact amount Mr. Smith gives, but "we wouldn't have a balanced budget if it wasn't for so-and-so."

People defer to them. People know who they are. In a Presbyterian church, you're not talking about a three, four, or five thousand congregation. The average church is probably run by eight or nine families. New people come in, but in the old guard they know what people are doing and who's doing what.

INTERVIEWER: I've had two pastors tell me that they don't know who the big givers are in their church.
PASTOR: I don't believe them. No. Well, I imagine there are some ministers who are so obtuse that they don't see the Mercedes sitting in the parking lot. And they don't see how the church members talk about some people. People change their tone of voice when they talk about them.

We were never able to resolve these issues. A presbytery executive gave us his view, which is valuable:

> I don't think all of the leadership or the accountability should come from the pastor. But somebody in the congregation ought to have the ministry of helping people think through their stewardship. In many churches that may be the pastor—particularly in smaller churches. It doesn't need to be the pastor; it could be a lay officer. But I think there needs to be somebody who knows what you give and who has the authority in the mind of the church to converse with you about your pledge. I would like to create a norm of some kind of accountability in all the churches. We realize that people are all at different stages in their journey. There's a lot of emphasis on getting people to grow in their stewardship. A lot of people will come in and start out giving a dollar a week, and they need to be kept aware that there ought to be some relationship between the amount of their income and the amount of their gift.
>
> I've heard stories from pastors that someone was giving a small amount because they literally didn't know any better. And when somebody explained the facts of life to them and what the median giving was, and what generous giving amounted to, with very little fuss they changed radically. It had just never occurred to them. They thought they were doing fine until somebody talked with them.

A Survey by John and Sylvia Ronsvalle

John and Sylvia Ronsvalle recently surveyed 97 pastors and 112 regional officials in Protestant mainline and conservative denominations.[1] The sample was composed of people who came to stewardship workshops and their friends, thus does not pretend to be representative. But its views are important. The researchers asked for agreement or disagreement on two statements: (1) "The pastor's knowledge of what individual members give to the church can be a helpful assessment tool of individual members' spiritual health." On this, 78 percent of the pastors and 82 percent of the regional officials agreed. Note that this statement does not say that pastors *should* look at individuals' giving because other arguments may counterbalance this one. But a reasonable inference is that these pastors and officials would favor having a pastor look. (2) "Most church members do not want the pastor to know how much individual members contribute to the church." Eighty-three percent of the pastors agreed, as did 79 percent of the regional officials.

It seems commonly agreed among pastors and officials that pastors would benefit from looking at individuals' giving, yet members are opposed. Why this difference? We can only guess that pastors derive additional confidence and empowerment from knowing individual giving, thus they argue for it. Members prefer to remain anonymous, possibly because the level of giving of many is embarrassingly low. It is also possible that a few big givers may want anonymity out of humility or out of a fear of damaging social relationships.

We conclude that the clergy would like to strengthen social reciprocity in giving (by removing anonymity) while many laity would like to minimize social reciprocity and detection. We would speculate that the laity most desiring anonymity would be those who feel no other strong motivation to give and who in fact give less.

Should We Recognize Big Gifts?

We found consensus among the pastors that donors of large gifts should not be thanked publicly except in a few circumstances. Yet attitudes varied on details. We asked a Presbyterian pastor if he would publicly recognize a large gift, for example $10,000 from Mrs. Jones.

No, I would never thank her publicly. I don't like any person or anything to be brought up in a very individualistic way. Basically we are a congregation and a community, and we are all in this together. It's not a performance; it's something that Mrs. Jones does.

We asked the same question of a Lutheran pastor.

PASTOR: We wouldn't announce a gift from Mrs. Jones. We would write her a letter. We'll say that anything she needs for her income tax is fine.
INTERVIEWER: Who knows about the gift? Just you and the finance committee?
PASTOR: Yes.
INTERVIEWER: Is there a general principle here about big gifts?
PASTOR: Big ones? Gifts are gifts! Grace is grace! You don't distinguish big ones and little ones! If we did, we'd be praising the 20 percent who usually support 60 percent of the budget. It's a very rare practice, if at all, in Lutheran churches to let people know who gave what big gifts. Well, the giver may tell other people.
The only place the givers are identified is on capital funds. Some churches have the practice of saying something like "The stained glass windows were given by X," and they put up plaques. We have a book that we keep on display in the narthex that tells who gave the pews and pulpit and so forth. But we make no big deal over it.
INTERVIEWER: Does it give the dollar amounts, like "Mr. and Mrs. Jones, $40,000 for the windows?"
PASTOR: Yes, it gives their names or the names of a whole group of people who went together for something like the windows. But never the dollar amount. If it's a banner in the church, or a chalice, or something in the sanctuary, we would have a dedication ceremony for it.
INTERVIEWER: Would you say "Mrs. Jones gave this?"
PASTOR: Well, in the bulletin we might, but we wouldn't use that as part of the occasion. But we do not make a big deal out of who gives what. It's not really for a theological reason; it just feels tacky. It's kind of the Jim and Tammy Faye Bakker approach. See, in the church we're all equal. We need to remember the agape feast in the New Testament, and we need to be sure that everyone is level at the foot of the cross. The same place.

We put the same question to a veteran Presbyterian pastor.

INTERVIEWER: Suppose a gift for $20,000 came in from Mrs. Jones. Would you announce that in church?
PASTOR: I would do what she requests.
INTERVIEWER: Some people may want to buy esteem with the gift.
PASTOR: Well, I would ask her if she wants it announced. What people often say is, "I want this to be an anonymous gift." If people say that, then not even the stewardship committee would know who it is.
INTERVIEWER: But you will know.
PASTOR: Yes, I'll know.
INTERVIEWER: If she really wanted it to be anonymous, she would find a way to give it that not even you would know.
PASTOR: Well, that's true. And we've had that. We had a lawyer come to us and hand us a check on his firm's account. He said it was from an anonymous donor. And we wrote a thank-you letter to his firm and asked him to pass it on. We had no idea who it came from.

This pastor argued that recognizing big givers encourages others to do the same.

PASTOR: As pastor I want to acknowledge the big gift and use the donor as an example, so others will make a major gift. A side effect is that the donor will get some social standing. And that's going to motivate maybe some other people to give. I believe what a secular fund raiser taught us, that you should publicize a big gift.

A Lutheran pastor told us that the millionaires in the parishes he has served tended to prefer capital gifts over large annual gifts. He said that they usually wanted recognition for their gifts.

INTERVIEWER: If Mrs. Jones gave $20,000 for, let us say, a chapel, would anybody know it?
PASTOR: Yes, everybody would know. But you wouldn't see "Jones Memorial Chapel" above the door.

We asked a Presbyterian pastor what he would do if Mrs. Jones gave him a check for $10,000.

PASTOR: The general policy of the church has been to announce that we have received a gift of $10,000 from one of our parishioners, but not to give the name.

INTERVIEWER: Why don't you say at some occasion, "Thanks to Mrs. Jones for the gift of $10,000 this year"?

PASTOR: Then I think there are all kinds of ways in which parishioners will begin to treat Mrs. Jones differently. Mrs. Jones will no doubt make the list of potential candidates for elder next time. Everybody has their ground rules. And we have them too. We do make it a practice of publishing it if we do receive special gifts, just to let people know that such things do happen. We give the name.

Two pastors told us that they favored having a periodic social gathering to which the biggest givers were invited. One Presbyterian pastor shared his experiences in several wealthy congregations:

PASTOR: In several congregations, when we were coming up to a stewardship season, I invited the top givers to the manse. I drew a line in the list and picked the top 5 percent. And I invited them to the manse just to thank them. I would say to them, "You know, if it hadn't been for givers like you this church would be in serious trouble."

INTERVIEWER: I assume they all know that they are in the top group.

PASTOR: Yes. And the whole congregation gets the word, too, that those people have been asked to the manse. The word gets around! I mean, it gets around!

INTERVIEWER: And you don't mind that people know that. Maybe it's a good thing.

PASTOR: Yes, it is. The next year around, there are people who deliberately pledge to get up into that area because they would like to be in that group. I make it a big deal. And at the gathering I don't push the budget or anything else. My wife usually fixes us a real nice refreshment. We stand around with some wine, the fireplace going, and all that. And at some time I'll say, "I want to take a few minutes to thank you for what you've done. You've given significantly. We're starting the stewardship campaign again, as usual, and I know all of you are going to come through with an increase because you do every year." That's all I say. And those people I can count on. Once a person gets into that, you don't have to dun them. They want to be there.

He explained his philosophy:

The pastor needs to know what this is all about and deliberately
pitch to it. For instance, I can see on the giving list the names of
people I know, who ought to be giving a lot more. And I will at
some time or other talk to that person because I think that it is a
measure of his or her commitment to Christ. I come right up and say
to them, "Look, I note that you are in this category of giving. And
you ought to think about that. Is there some problem, that you can't
give more?" I'll talk to that person that straight. Now there are
some who don't like that. But nine times out of ten, I'm convinced,
people want to know what is expected of them. That is almost a
universal.

Another Presbyterian pastor had similar views on recognition of
gifts:

Periodically we have a reception or a dinner for the major givers
and thank them. . . . Lifting up somebody who has been magnani-
mous can be an inspiration for someone else to do the same. So in
our endowment fund, if the gift is over $1,000, we list the funds in
the annual report by name. And if there is a memorial gift, there's
got to be public recognition for that because you're memorializing
somebody.

Other pastors did not agree with the idea of having private parties
for large givers. An Episcopal priest:

I wouldn't do that. The people in this parish whose opinions I respect a lot would be appalled at that. They would be appalled at
that method of trying to get better giving and separating out the
ones who are the really big givers. The people here wouldn't stand
for it, so I wouldn't want to do it either.

He went on to say that his church's practice regarding big gifts has
evolved to fit the style of its people.

This is a well-to-do community. A lot of folks here have a family

tradition to give large gifts to places that they support such as the
art museum, the zoo, or the church. They don't need the public
recognition. I think people want to hear from me, though. I get a
sense that they want the rector to know that they gave and to be
thanked by the rector. If I don't write a thank-you note, people are
hurt and very upset.

We talked to a Presbyterian pastor about the church we described
above where the pastor invited the biggest givers to a private party. He
reacted strongly:

PASTOR: That makes me sick to my stomach! Don't let that kind of thing
happen in front of me.
INTERVIEWER: Why are you against it?
PASTOR: For the simple reason that the news gets out and they're going to
get elitist treatment. No matter how you try to convince people that, no,
they're not going to get any better treatment than the rest, they won't
believe you. And they're probably right!

Issues Related to Reciprocity with God

Does God enter into reciprocity with individuals? Does God reward
givers for their gifts? This is a question pertinent to persons who trust in
a personal God, but not for everyone. For people who are uncertain
about their idea of God or uncertain about whether God relates to individual humans, it is not an issue. Thus for the moment our attention is
limited to church members who trust in a relationship with God.

We heard clashing viewpoints about whether God rewards givers,
and for a moment we entertained a hope of clarifying the question
through exegesis of biblical texts. After all, the preachers who said yes
and the preachers who said no were both basing their arguments on the
Bible, and possibly Bible study could clarify the matter. But we quickly
abandoned the idea. We observed how preachers drew very diverse theological lessons from the Bible, and we saw that proponents of any one
interpretation do not accept others. The preachers we studied accorded
little authority to scholars who held different viewpoints. All we as researchers can do is to report the different teachings we heard.

Does God reward givers? A prior question is: Does God reward *any* humans in *any* way? The answer from the Bible is surely yes. Biblical passages abound that speak of rewards for human behavior, either individual or collective. Living in hope of future reward is at the center of Christianity. Passages promising rewards abound, especially in the Gospels. Here are some famous ones:

> Blessed are the meek, for they will inherit the earth. . . . Blessed are those who are persecuted for righteousness' sake, for theirs is the kingdom of heaven. . . . Rejoice and be glad, for your reward is great in heaven, for in the same way they persecuted the prophets who were before you. Matthew 5:5-12

> When you give alms, do not let your left hand know what your right hand is doing, so that your alms may be done in secret; and your Father who sees in secret will reward you. Matthew 6:3-4

> Do not judge, and you will not be judged; do not condemn, and you will not be condemned. Forgive, and you will be forgiven; give, and it will be given to you. A good measure, pressed down, shaken together, running over, will be put into your lap; for the measure you give will be the measure you get back. Luke 6:37-38

From the Epistles:

> The one who sows sparingly will also reap sparingly, and the one who sows bountifully will also reap bountifully. . . . You will be enriched in every way for your great generosity, which will produce thanksgiving to God through us. 2 Corinthians 9:6-12

> You reap whatever you sow. If you sow to your own flesh, you will reap corruption from the flesh; but if you sow to the Spirit, you will reap eternal life from the Spirit. So let us not grow weary in doing what is right, for we will reap at harvest-time. Galatians 6:7-9

May Christians give in hopes of future reward? The New Testament texts either state or imply that the answer is yes. Can humans buy salvation and heavenly blessings by their actions, either good works or monetary gifts? Here the question becomes complex. Most Christian doctrine says that salvation is by grace and faith, not by good works, and not available for purchase through financial gifts. Yet the sermons we heard vacillated on this point and sometimes said contradictory things. To explain, we need to distinguish two types of rewards.

Are Monetary Gifts Rewarded by God?

We heard several sermons saying that God, in one way or other, rewards givers for financial gifts. The most direct teaching is that monetary gifts to God will be repaid in cash by God. This is an uncommon theme, and we have heard it only from television evangelists. The most common Gospel passage is Mark 10:29-31, which says that followers of Christ will "receive a hundredfold now in this age."

More common is the message that gifts are repaid through spiritual blessings. We heard this mainly in evangelical and pentecostal churches. For example, an Assemblies of God pastor:

> The fact of the matter is, you cannot be victorious as a Christian, you cannot be overcoming, you cannot be the kind of disciple who falls under the lordship of Jesus Christ if you are selfish with the funds that God has entrusted to you. If you take from the resources that God has given you, and be faithful and obedient to him on a simple level, then you will begin to see him at work in your life in many ways that will enrich you, that will cause you to mature, to grow, and yes, we as a congregation will then be able to do so much more for Christ and his kingdom.

The same preacher on a different Sunday spelled out what will happen if someone does *not* tithe. If you don't tithe, he preached, it will catch up with you later.

> If you don't give God his due, I can promise you that sooner or later it will show up in problems in your life. This is one of the spiritual principles of life.

An evangelical pastor in a different denomination said that although he never preaches that God will repay Christians for monetary gifts, he knows other preachers (he mentioned Baptists) who do. He disapproves of this, but it occurs widely. He told of pastor friends who tell their people that "God will get his tithe one way or the other." If they don't give it freely, God will take it from them later in hospital bills or financial troubles. For these preachers the doctrine of reciprocity with God carries both hope and threat.

An Assemblies of God preacher in the South declared in a sermon that following God's commandments and giving our lives to God is not just something that we do for altruistic purposes. No. It is something we do *in our own interest.* Any intelligent person, once he or she understands what is at stake, would do it. It is for our own good! It is really the only way to live, because God is in command of the world, and God will determine how our life goes.

The sermon continued:

We who have given our lives to Christ can live with confidence that God will take care of us. It is in our interest to love God and keep his commandments, including tithing. It is in our interest not to love the things of the world because God is in command. This is not just a fire insurance policy to keep us out of hell! This is a promise to us for eternity. Once we give our lives to God we can be assured from God's promises that he will guide our lives for eternity.

The most common scriptural text on tithing is Malachi 3:10: "Bring the full tithe into the storehouse, so that there may be food in my house, and thus put me to the test, says the Lord of hosts; see if I will not open the windows of heaven for you and pour down for you an overflowing blessing." We heard several sermons stressing that tithes will result in blessings. A person who gives his or her life to God and contributes a tithe can have total confidence in God's word. Give a tithe and you can have freedom from fear about the future.

Mainline pastors sounded different. They all agreed that God does not repay or reward specific individuals for monetary gifts. For example, we asked a Presbyterian pastor if God rewards givers.

PASTOR: I can answer that: no. That's not the kind of God I understand. I don't think God rewards or punishes people by whether they give or not, or whether they stand aside in a tragedy or get involved.

INTERVIEWER: Once I was in a Sunday school class—not in a Presbyterian church—and the people there were talking very candidly. One asked, "What do you get if you give?" and another answered, "A check mark." He meant in the Book of Life. The others all nodded in agreement.

PASTOR: That's not where I am. I would never say that!

INTERVIEWER: So God doesn't reciprocate.

PASTOR: No. That's not the motivation. That's not what giving is about. It's not what Jesus was talking about either.

INTERVIEWER: It would seem to be human nature because life is so short and uncertain, and because God is powerful and eternal, to perhaps do good things and make a deal somehow.

PASTOR: Well, of course it's a strong tradition. One of the crises over that came when Martin Luther dealt with the indulgences, which were all around that same subject. There are a lot of people today who still believe that.

INTERVIEWER: I want you to act as an observer of the Presbyterian Church in the U.S. Do you hear pastors talking about God rewarding you for your gifts?

PASTOR: Yes, I've heard it among Presbyterians. Yes.

INTERVIEWER: Was that from some oddball, or is it a major theme?

PASTOR: I have a sense that it's probably more true than I would like to think. Because there's still an awful lot of pastors who take it to the other extreme—that if you're not in church, God's not going to bless you. I can't handle any of that. That's just not my theology. But I do hear it, unfortunately, and I hear it from Presbyterians.

INTERVIEWER: See if you agree with this: Protestant people who believe God rewards givers will actually end up giving more.

PASTOR: My guess is yes, that would be true.

INTERVIEWER: Possibly a Presbyterian pastor who is worried about meeting the budget might be tempted to preach that God will reward givers.

PASTOR: (laugh) I think that's true. But I think it collapses in the long run. Supposing I preach that "If you give, God will bless you and God will take care of you." So some guy gives well. And then two days later some idiot fatally shoots his wife. He comes to me and says, "Why did God do that? I've given, and you told me that if I gave, God would take care of me and bless me." What answer do you give the guy? I mean, that is a bad cycle to get into, when you start saying that kind of stuff—whether it's about stewardship and how much you give, or whether it's how many times you go to church, or how many times you pray.

We asked a Lutheran pastor if Christians buy anything from God with their gifts.

PASTOR: That's a tough one, particularly tough for Lutherans, with our preoccupation with justification by grace through faith, grace junkies that we are. We have real problems with the "r word" [reward], the idea that God rewards certain human behavior. That is so antithetical to Brother Martin and the whole Lutheran tradition that we choke over it.
INTERVIEWER: One author I've read says that parishioners who believe there is a reward actually do give more money.
PASTOR: I'm sure! It's kind of like an investment!
INTERVIEWER: It follows then that people trying to keep churches going will have a great temptation to preach that.
PASTOR: Yes, I think that's a great temptation. But I think it has been shattered for a number of parishioners of mine over the years by the unpredictability of personal tragedy. They ask, "Why did God allow this to happen to me, pastor? After all, my late husband was a pillar of the church, and so was I." You see, she gave generously. So that makes me uncomfortable. My father once sold life insurance, so the insurance analogy is very real to me. I think it is a trivialization of the grace of God to get too far into the insurance metaphor.

We asked a presbytery executive if pastors should say to their people, "If you tithe, God will take care of your needs, not only today but forever." His response was clear.

EXECUTIVE: No. For anyone coming from a Presbyterian or Lutheran background, that would be sheer heresy. Because salvation is a sheer gift, undeserved, the whole idea that God takes care of you to the extent that you deserve it violates the very core of our faith. In the Bible it says, "While we were yet sinners, Christ died for us." Salvation is an undeserved gift that reflects God's unconditional love. And the whole idea of conditional love, that God is nice to us in response to our niceness to God, so that we basically earn God's love by being generous, is heresy.
INTERVIEWER: So God's not in the reward.
PASTOR: God is in it, but not in that simplistic reward and punishment way. God is in it, I think, in terms of what God has revealed about

God's self. And what it means to be an authentic human being, to be made in the image of God and live a faithful life, to love in the way that God has loved us.

We asked an Episcopal pastor whether God rewards givers.

No. I don't say that at all. I don't say if you give, God will do better for you. One televangelist would say, "Give more money and you'll get a Cadillac next year." I hopefully don't give that theology. What I say is, build up the relationship from your end. That's where I leave it. I don't say there will be a *quid pro quo* because what if someone loses a family member or gets sick and says, I tithed, so how come God didn't fulfill God's part of the bargain? . . . I know that a lot of quack preachers give that message. They say this is how God operates. There are many writers in the Bible who get into that. I think some of the psalms say that. But the more advanced or theologically mature writers in the biblical literature don't say that at all. Job doesn't say that. Isaiah doesn't say that. Most of the prophets don't say that. With Jesus, there is one quote where he says, "Give and it will be given to you, measure for measure, pressed down and overflowing." For the most part, though, Jesus fights greed. Over and over again what he has to say is that the worst condition of the heart is greed. To show that you are not enslaved to your possessions, give even more abundantly. So I don't think he says you will be rewarded in kind if you give.

Do Monetary Gifts Produce Spiritual Rewards Apart from God's Action?

Pastors often said that financial giving is rewarding even apart from specific reciprocity with God. Giving enhances life, produces satisfaction, and adds to happiness. This reward is conceptually separate from any social esteem from others derived through social reciprocity (discussed above). Giving was often described to us as a spiritual discipline or spiritual exercise that has its own benefits. One Presbyterian pastor:

PASTOR: I don't think God rewards people by what they give. The reward in giving is what it has done for me! When my wife and I see something that we've been able to accomplish in this particular community, it makes us feel real good that we've been involved. And when we travel overseas, like we did in the Middle East, it felt good to see what our denomination has done for these people with the money that we gave them.

INTERVIEWER: So that's the reward for giving.

PASTOR: The reward is altruism, or whatever you want to call it. It's there in the whole understanding of the generosity of the Spirit. And the feeling of community.

We asked a Lutheran pastor what God does for givers:

What God gives you is the feeling of well-being because you have given. That's a part of who we are as God's church. Here's an analogy. Part of the problem in marriages today is that some people think, "By getting married, I'm going to have my spouse make me happy," a kind of reward point of view. If they do, they'll never be happy, and the marriage isn't going to be much. But if they go into the marriage saying, "By giving myself to that other person, I am rewarded," then they find that they receive back. But that's not the reason they give. By giving you receive. It's just that simple and biblical. But you can't turn it into a reward system. The minute you start turning it into a reward system, you lose it.

A Presbyterian pastor:

PASTOR: There have been some studies done. *Psychology Today* has published some studies, as other publications have, demonstrating that people who are giving and who love others are healthier, feel better about themselves, and live longer. So there is a reward to a life of benevolence. There is a penalty to a life of selfishness. We talk about those people being "little" because we observe that that is what they become. Loving others is a better way to live your life. You don't look for happiness, you look for ways to serve others to make *them* happy, and you'll discover that you're the happiest one.

INTERVIEWER: Why do the big givers give so much?

PASTOR: They feel great! They feel really good! You can get high on giving and you can get high on stewardship. It's a lot healthier than getting high on drugs.

A Lutheran minister told about a parishioner:

PASTOR: I know a lot of tithers. There was a retired postal clerk in the church who told me once that he "was challenged to tithe years ago, which I did! Now I'm up to 17 percent." And he added, "It's wonderful."
INTERVIEWER: Why does he feel that? Because God has blessed him?
PASTOR: Because he's fulfilled from within, I think. He has accepted the responsibility of serving rather than being served. And he delights in serving others and taking on that role of servant.
INTERVIEWER: Does God look at him differently from another guy who doesn't do that?
PASTOR: I don't think so. But the person looks at God differently.

A Methodist pastor:

PASTOR: I think there is a great reward in giving. And it comes in all kinds of surprising ways. I'm not one who says, "If you give, then God is going to reward you, and this is the way you're going to be rewarded." But I think as one learns to live a life in stewardship on behalf of others, changes occur in one's whole perception of life and the world, and one's life is dramatically altered. That's what one gets out of it. . . . The reward is a change in how one sees the world and how one relates to that world. Part of it is a paradox in that life itself is much more full and much more complete when one recognizes the incredible interdependence of all human beings in this world. So I know that if one of the students in a particular school in the inner city is suffering, *I* suffer because of that. And if that student can make good changes in his or her life, then *I* am blessed by that as well.
INTERVIEWER: Well, it seems to take a specialized perception, no?
PASTOR: It does! It takes those of us in the church helping each other to make the commitment to come to that point. And part of the joy is being part of a congregation that tries to do this.

A Lutheran pastor:

PASTOR: I don't preach too much about reward, and when I do, it's apologetic. For example, I'll say, "I need you to know that there are a whole lot of folks here who give far more than the average, and a number of good things happen to them. It's just been their experience. And I'm one of them. Giving becomes an adventure rather than a duty. I want to tell you what's happened to some of us. Our experience is that a life that matures in stewardship and Christian philanthropy and giving seems to experience no want!"

The interviewer questioned this pastor's view because the pastor said that God does not reward individual givers. He clarified:

PASTOR: I've got a dialectic in my mind. There are rewards, but you can't guarantee them. There are rewards to be experienced in stewardship, to which I personally give testimony out of my own life and the lives of others who have shared with me.
INTERVIEWER: What kind of reward is it?
PASTOR: Well, I think initially it's simply not being in want financially, of those things for which finances are necessary. I think it's a self-fulfilling prophecy in terms of relationship and commitment to God. It's as though the more you commit, the more committed you feel! The more you move closer to what you understand God's will to be, the more you feel like you're in the hands of God and his will! I think it's also an emotional peace of mind. I think it's an integrating experience, that which helps create a sense of personal and family wholeness.

Issues Related to Giving to the Extended Self

The third motive we identified in chapter 3 was that of giving to the extended self, or more simply, giving out of love. It is strong. The more the members love the church, the more they will give.

The main practical issue that we heard in this regard is love *of what*: Is it love of the pastor, love of the church, or love of the heritage? One test that shows where the love is strongest is to see how the level of giving changes when a person moves to a different town and joins a different church. We asked a Presbyterian pastor about this:

INTERVIEWER: Suppose a good church member moves to another town and selects a new Presbyterian church. Does that person's giving start at zero or does it stay at the same level? What is your experience? Is it dependent on whether that person likes the pastor?

PASTOR: My experience has been that the giving will stay at the level it was. It might change after the person has been there and discovers a few things. I've heard people say things like, "I'm not happy with the new pastor and the program here." But eventually they will give the same amount of money, but give it to different places. Their level of giving will stay the same. That's my experience.

We put the same question to a Lutheran pastor. He agreed:

My guess is that if the new pastor in the new church proves credible and authentic, and cares about a new member, that person's commitment to the Lord will bring him or her into that church at as high a level as it was in the previous church. I think there is an immature kind of stewardship that's based on personal affection, and maybe as many as 25 to 40 percent of the people are at that point. But the majority of experienced church members will soon be at the same giving level in the new church.

We asked a presbytery executive if members' giving depends greatly on how they like the pastor.

I think there are both kinds. I've known some who, if he or she is a committed tither, always tithe. Some people are clear that they join the church, not the pastor. Other people have that all mixed up. The healthy church attitude is that giving is not simply determined by the personality cult of the pastor. If you join the church you become disciples of Jesus, not disciples of Reverend Doctor So-and-So.

Another Presbyterian pastor explained that he tried to constrain people's devotion to particular ministers:

With preaching, never in my ministry have I ever put on the bulletin board or in the newspaper who was preaching. And if people call on Sunday morning and ask who is preaching, we answer in a graceful way, "We don't announce that." God is to be worshipped in this place, not preachers.

An Episcopal rector commented:

I think that liking the programs is one of the biggest motivations for why people really give here. I've had people say they are cutting back their pledge because they don't like something the national church is doing or they don't think they'll give a lot because we don't have a youth worker. People will give to a program they like. And if the money isn't being used for programs they like, they will let us know.

A Presbyterian pastor stressed the concept of ownership:

My role as pastor in the stewardship campaign is an ongoing, never-ending role to try to create a sense of connection between people's lives and what goes on here. When they sense they have a connection here, then they sense that this is their church, and that is the ownership that people are talking about.

Issues Related to Giving out of Thankfulness

In our experiences the topic of giving out of thankfulness came up most often in conversations of *what should be*. It came up less often in discussions of actual reality. Protestant clergy pointed out over and over that thankfulness should be a central motivation experienced by all of us.

Let us be clear that gratitude is different from reciprocity, in that the gift is given without an expectation of future return; it is the final act of a chain of reciprocity actions in the past. It is different from giving out of love, but only slightly so; we cannot imagine a substantial gift being given out of gratitude if there is no love for the recipient.

Several times we heard an analogy to giving to one's college alma mater. Many people of middle age or older feel gratitude for what their college did for their lives, and this motivates them to give to it. Similarly, many people feel that their church has served them and their families well, and they give out of a sense of appreciation. They may feel that God has been good to them, and they give to God out of appreciation. A Presbyterian layperson commented:

I was born with gifts given from God, and in my relationship with God, I want to give back to God by giving to God's programs. I had to find the way to do that, find the church, and find the way to make that selection.

Another Presbyterian layperson:

It's returning God's gifts. I feel that, being fortunate and in a position to give, the church becomes a vehicle for me to acknowledge that and to channel some of that to others.

People who have been equally blessed by God or by their church will not always feel equally thankful for that. A feeling of thankfulness is an aspect of personality and character, quite apart from the amount of one's blessings. Each community has diverse persons, some "graspers" and some "givers." Whether or not a person feels thankful depends on upbringing and training.

A Methodist minister estimated that thankfulness was not a strong motive in financial giving in his church:

Maybe I'm being a pessimist here, but I just don't think that thankfulness really motivates our people to give to this church. I think that years ago maybe that entered in, but I don't think it does any more. Maybe my vision is too myopic, but that's all I can see. More often, if the church is serving me as a member and meets my needs, fine, I'll give. Or if I'm retired, then I do it out of tradition or loyalty or whatever.

We came to conclude that thankfulness is a long-term thing, a matter of how we see other people. The difference between a thankful person and a thankless person is a basic trait. We put this question to a Presbyterian pastor:

INTERVIEWER: Let us take an example. Millionaire A gives $20,000 to the church. He feels good. Millionaire B spends $20,000 on himself. He builds a cottage. He feels good too. Maybe the difference is just a matter of people's upbringing or tendencies. There's no *theological* reason why Millionaire A would have to give the $20,000 to the church except that sometime in his life somebody has made the connection, so he feels good.

PASTOR: That's right. It has to be our upbringing and how we've been taught. And we're getting into a generation of folks now, the kids, who haven't had that upbringing. And bringing them into a life of stewardship is going to be a real challenge.

For Reflection and Discussion

1. Do you agree or disagree with this statement from the Ronsvalle's survey: "The pastor's knowledge of what individual members give to the church can be a helpful assessment tool of individual members' spiritual health"? Why? Do you agree or disagree with the Ronsvalle's statement, "Most church members do not want the pastor to know how much individual members contribute to the church"? Why?

2. Who, if anyone, do you think should take responsibility for talking with members about their giving?

3. Does your congregation have policies and procedures for recognizing special gifts? If so, do the policies and procedures vary depending on the size of the gift? If your congregation does not have policies and procedures in place, how would you recommend your church respond to special gifts?

4. Do you think God rewards givers? Why or why not? What do you think members of your congregation believe about this? Beginning with the position you think most of your members hold, what two or three points would you raise in a sermon to try to persuade them to change their minds about the matter?

5. How do you answer the question, Do monetary gifts produce spiritual rewards apart from God's action? Why do you believe your view is correct?

CHAPTER 5

Stewardship versus Fund Raising

Stewardship and fund raising are two distinctive frames of mind among church members. Here we will describe each as we observed them in action. Stewardship is exemplified by Steve, a software engineer for an electronics corporation and a member of his Presbyterian church's stewardship committee.

> I am giving to this church because God is working through it. I'm not giving to the pastor but to God. The necessary thing for every Christian is to elevate his or her thinking to a sense of trust in and dependency on God, and one way to bring this about is to "disable" the things that inhibit my sense of trust in and dependence on the Creator.

The pastor of Steve's church has striven for twenty-five years to make stewardship the governing ideal of his church, and a quarter of a century later the results are evident not only in an impressive array of buildings, ministries, and a million-dollar-plus budget, but also in the viewpoints of the congregational members we interviewed. Steve is typical of many members of this church who see that stewardship decisions come to be made throughout daily life. Steve likens making stewardship decisions to buying a new car:

STEVE: A decision can be made at the dealership showroom—do we really want to buy this car now? I think it really grows on you. It's not something you get into right away. It's the outcome of faith commitment over time.
INTERVIEWER: Do you expect a return from God for such a faith commitment?

STEVE: No. You don't cut deals with God. Stewardship is a response to what you have already been given. The benefit is an increased sense of your dependency on God.

INTERVIEWER: Do you expect to be safeguarded by God?

STEVE: No. God may send you a blow and know it will help you grow in faith and understanding. Disasters can be for your spiritual growth. Protection? No.

In our talks with pastors, we asked them how they conceived of stewardship and how they distinguished stewardship programs from fund raising. How did they frame stewardship without making it sound like just another way of getting money? We found many pastors wrestling with these issues. In our talks with lay members we asked how they perceived stewardship and what it requires in their lives.

Some of the pastors and laypersons we quote here belong to evangelical churches, in particular, Southern Baptist and Assemblies of God. Others are Presbyterians, Lutherans, Methodists, Episcopalians, or members of the United Church of Christ. All, regardless of denomination, grapple with stewardship issues in one way or another. Their experiences offer lessons for pastors and lay members: How do we, within our own traditions, encourage giving time, talent, and treasure from ourselves and our members? What kinds of commitment does all this require, and how do we elicit that commitment?

Let us be specific about the definitions of fund raising and stewardship.

Fund Raising as a Secular Enterprise

Secular fund raising is a specialty in the field of marketing. It relies on a host of techniques that can be observed at any fund-raising convention: mailing lists, computerized prospect sorting systems, direct-mail printing, magazine advertisements, and more. Fund-raising professionals have accumulated a stock of wisdom about human motives and about how people can be motivated to give. Central to fund raising are the following:

* First, most gifts in the United States are given not by corporations or foundations but by individuals.

During the 1980s over 80 percent of all private-sector gifts were from individuals. Personal contacts and personal solicitation are the most effective method of fund raising. In the most successful approach, a respected volunteer visits a few of his or her friends (in a typical campaign, about four or five persons), speaks enthusiastically of the cause and of how he or she has already given, and asks for help. This is the basic process. Telephone calls to friends are less effective, mailings even less so. Fund raising implies social reciprocity either hoped for or explicitly offered by the asker, as described above in chapter 3. The interplay of social pressure and reciprocity benefits most people and rarely offends anyone because everyone in the community knows the rules of the game. In fact, appeals are often made in a kind of "sporting" atmosphere. Jewish groups commonly enjoy holding fund-raising parties during which clever ribbing and repartee goes on. A similar method is often at work in churches during capital campaigns: "Hey Charlie, anyone who can afford that new golf cart can come up with a check for the church!"

• A willing and capable volunteer group is essential.

Veteran fund raisers know that volunteers must be discovered, nurtured, and loved over a period of years. A solid core of experienced volunteers who reappear from year to year is simply invaluable. They must also be included in the process of designing the campaign and its goals, including specific uses for the money. That is, they must feel ownership for the cause.

• A written "case statement" is needed.

It needs to say, What will the money be used for? Where is it going? The positive must be emphasized, not the negative. For example, campaigns will founder if they emphasize how *needy* the organization is. Other motivational sources must be tapped. In *Fund-Raising Fundamentals*, James Greenfield suggests that donors may well begin work "with a glow of enlightened self-interest," but in time can be helped to see that they are participating in a worthy cause, are joined with others in a common purpose, and are helping an organization deserving their confidence.[1]

•   Donors must be recognized.

Big donors need to be thanked publicly. Everyone must be thanked without delay and kept informed during the following year on the uses to which the money is put.

Stewardship Is a Distinctive Approach

Unlike secular fund raising, stewardship is deeply rooted in theology. It is not just a fund-raising strategy disguised under a religious veneer. Stewardship embraces a theology of acknowledgment: humans are to recognize that God created all the goods of this world. We do not own the world and its good things, but we are stewards or caretakers of these goods and are responsible for their proper use during our limited time on earth. The goods include our time, our treasure, and our talent. Framed this way, stewardship becomes a way of life. It is not simply a way of deciding how to use one's wealth or treasure, but involves "Nothing less than a complete lifestyle, a total accountability and responsibility before God. Stewardship is what we do after we say we believe, that is, after we give our love, loyalty, and trust to God, from whom each and every aspect of our lives comes as a gift."[2]

As an example of stewardship theology, the Evangelical Lutheran Church in America makes available a two-page "Financial Stewardship Strategy" guide. It is typical of statements issued by denominational offices of stewardship. It opens by acknowledging that "the church faces a crisis in mission funding and in stewardship:"

> We face many challenges. There is much more competition for financial support among our members. The church is no longer at the center, and automatic loyalty cannot be assumed. There are great attractions for using and spending money in a variety of ways. There is also great opportunity as we seek to assist our members in thoughtful and responsible stewardship, and as we seek to advance the mission of Christ's church through sufficient funding for mission.

The statement emphasizes five points. If any one of these is missing in a congregation embarking on a stewardship strategy, the response can suffer:

1. The people need a faith perspective with clear articulation of the purpose of the church. This faith is Gospel-rooted and "has the ability to shape and transform us. . . . It is grounded in scripture, and the believer is constantly stirred up. A generous and thankful response is the mark of someone who is anchored in this faith."

2 . The people must believe in mission. The church exists "to announce the Good News of what God has done in Jesus Christ to all the world. . . This mission is central to the believer and has the power to change and save lives."

3. Believers need to trust the network of organizational entities that make up the church—congregations, synods, the denominational organization, and other church agencies. Believers are asked to hold these "partners" trustworthy in the way they handle finances and not to constrict their vision to only their local congregations.

4. The times call for leaders—both lay and clergy—who are bold, not timid, in the arena of stewardship. Leaders teach by example "and through their public proclamation." They are visible and they motivate. "Leaders model behavior that is carefully observed and often followed by members."

5. Discipleship includes participation through "our time, energy, prayers, and financial resources." People are to be invited "to challenge conventional wisdom and follow instead the way of the cross"; they are "encouraged to respond with offerings as an act of worship, as well as respond to specific opportunities for directed giving."

In congregations, specific strategies of encouraging giving are less important than "a healthy congregational system." A healthy congregation has:

- engaging preaching and lively worship
- an orientation to the future with intentional planning

- a strong commitment to evangelistic outreach
- an ability to manage conflict creatively.[3]

Although statements of ideals such as this one provide inspiration and guidance, we found that pastors vary a great deal in their conception of stewardship and in how much they emphasized it.

Stewardship: Pastors' Perspectives

The pastors we talked with were unanimous: stewardship is a multi-year educational effort, and nobody should expect short-term effects. No stewardship program lasting a few weeks can be expected to show sustained results. It is true that a new approach or a more vigorous program may increase pledges in one year, but it cannot nourish substantial growth year after year.

We heard different views on stewardship programs. Everyone we spoke with agreed that their churches needed increases in pledges over those of the past year, but not everyone endorsed trying a new program each year in hopes of raising pledges. Several pastors told us that this short-term campaign mentality is self-defeating. It tends to involve too much pressure on the church members, and it fails to teach stewardship as an integral part of Christian living. These pastors were uninterested in having stewardship committees that saw their job as only two or three months long, that is, putting on a campaign in hopes of going over the top, then resting until the next fall. Stewardship is more than just getting money from members' pockets into the church treasury; if that is all it is, everyone in the church will soon sense it and will resist the whole effort. People will say, "There they go again." No one likes salesmanship or pressure.

Church consultant Kennon Callahan argues that stewardship programs should be planned for four years, not just for one year. If an outside consultant is hired, it should be for a four-year period because a long period of time is needed for stewardship teaching to sink in. The pastors we talked with agreed. The effects of stewardship are broader than just money and include spiritual growth and richer human relationships. Stewardship training needs to be seen as part of training for Christian living. It needs to help Christians grow in faith and spiritual

maturity. It aims to enrich the lives of members while enriching the
ministries of the church.[4]

Stewardship, then, is part of the total spiritual training and upbuild-
ing of the congregation. One UCC pastor noted how opposed stewardship is to the adulation of money in our culture:

> I like to root stewardship in the fact that God wants to give to us,
> and it's only by opening our lives up to him that he's able to do
> that. And one of the ways we open our lives to him is by stopping
> the worship of money—by giving what our culture teaches us to
> hoard. It's always a challenge to find new ways of talking about
> stewardship.

A pastor of a church outstanding for its stewardship program:

> It's more biblical to talk about stewardship as it is in Scripture than
> to talk about your church's needs. The concept here is that every-
> thing belongs to God. Everything you have in the world is a gift to
> you. And we make that the foundation of our thinking rather than,
> "How much should I give?" We come naked into the world, so
> everything we have is a gift. As Christians we are gifted and re-
> deemed. This goes against what society says, and we have to bang
> away at it every year against the idea of "what's mine is mine."

Personal growth was a stewardship ideal we heard about frequently.
If church members are to be followers of Christ, they must open themselves to grow in every way—mentally, emotionally, spiritually. In
reality, people are at all different stages in the journey. Stewardship is
a part of growth. In the words of one pastor, "Our task is to help you
people grow in the mind of Jesus. . . . Five years from now you're going
to be a different person from the one you are now."

Preaching this growth ideal means challenging people. Christians
need to reverse their individualistic attitudes and to predicate giving, as
one pastor put it,

> upon the belief that we are just managers and stewards. We don't
> control everything. Yes, society says that we spend our time, our
> money, our energy on self and that happiness comes out of serving

self. The church is countercultural in that respect, believing that in order to be effective Christians, we must serve others.

Put simply: Stewardship is the fruit of faith, and building up faith and spirituality will increase financial giving. Don't try to make short-cuts. A Southern Baptist pastor told us about his church:

Here members *think* about giving and try to be as responsible as they can, whereas in so many mainline churches church giving is treated more or less like a monthly credit card bill. You don't think about "can I give more" or "how much should I give?" You just make your pledge and gripe about it to your wife, but you do it because you said you were going to do it. Here we constantly make it a spiritual discipline. It isn't cut and dried. The people here have to grapple with it, wrestle with it, every time they give. "Can I give more? Is there something more I could do to help? What is God telling me?"

Stewardship, then, as these pastors see it, does involve a yearly campaign, but more importantly it involves an ongoing effort to educate the congregation about returning to God the gifts each has been given. The result is life lived more fully. This is the reward. A Presbyterian pastor:

Loving others is a better way to live your life. Everyone's out there trying to find out "who I am, what's important in life, what I should be doing so I'll be happy." You should not look for happiness so much as you should look for ways to serve others and make them happy, and you'll discover that you're the happiest one.

While pastors agreed with this basic concept of stewardship, they disagreed on specifics and approaches. They told us of methods they have developed. For example, a Baptist pastor:

I preach stewardship sermons four or six times a year. I try not to preach, "We're out of money. Give more." I try to be much more intentional and very biblical. I try to use humor in the sermons to disarm people—since stewardship is an area in which people can

really get mousy . . . I deal with it biblically and I am not judg-
mental. I am positive, encouraging, and motivational, but I make a
strong rationale that this is a *positive expression* to God that we are
thankful. I present stewardship as a part of our Christian life, part of
our response to God's grace. God's grace affects us in a lot of ways,
but one way is that we try to reflect back our gratitude through our
life and our priorities and show appreciation for what God has done.

A Presbyterian pastor in California talked about his current stewardship drive:

An additional element this year is prayer. Our stewardship response
card has a place where people commit that they will pray, they will
care (which is using their gifts and talents), and then there's the
financial. But we emphasize overall that this is a response to God's
love, that it's something we do out of gratitude. Throughout the
year we do talk a lot about people using their gifts and talents; we
talk a lot about spiritual gifts, about finding out how you're wired
deep down inside and how God has gifted you, trying to encourage
and help people discover what their giftedness is and how all that
might coincide with ministries in the church.

Four other important topics were brought up by pastors:

1.   Stewardship requires a vision for the congregation. Several pastors
were quick to distinguish stewardship from exhortations simply to give
more. At the heart of stewardship was a distinctive *vision*:

My focus is not on the budget and we don't have a thermometer in
the foyer or a victory celebration afterwards because you never
"arrive" at Christian stewardship. . . . If you make stewardship a
bigger thing than money, and make it discipleship, a life commitment, not just financial, then you give people something big to grab
onto.

The same pastor, noting his large church plant and its manifold
ministries, explained:

To talk of the needs of this church was ludicrous. . . . I was embarrassed to talk this way. I know we need a lot, but why, when we
have so much? So now I talk about what we need to give to be
faithful disciples of the Lord Jesus, not what the church needs.
More important is what I need to do with my resources, my life, as
an appropriate response to what Christ has done in my life. So I
very seldom talk about need. . . . It's not fund raising we're into
here, it's vision raising. The Lord has given this church so much.
This congregation is blessed beyond what most churches could
begin to imagine. And not just for two or three years, but for decades. We need to respond in a big-time way to the blessings God
has bestowed on this church. And I find too many churches are still
focusing on this budget idea.

For another pastor the idea of vision was equivalent to what the
church is all about:

Let's call it vision casting, so we know who we are and what we're
about. And second is the whole relational issue, so people feel con-
fident in the pastor and his team and the board—a sense of confidence that we have a vision and the pastor and board are leading
toward that vision. And the third thing is consistency. The people
need to know where you are going. One church I know of changed
direction two or three different times, and that church has basically
evaporated. It almost disappeared. You can't first say that our emphasis is family ministry and then the next week, we're going to
be just an evangelistic center with big rallies. When this pastor
changed emphases, the people just sat down on him because what
he wanted to do was not what drew them in the first place.

2.   Stewardship theology encourages giving out of thankfulness and out
of a vision that everything we have comes from God. Veteran pastors
told us that it takes a long time to get this idea across, and not everyone
will understand it. The strength of this motive depends on the theological vision about the gifts we have received and what our response should
be. It is a vision not easily grasped by people new in the faith or weak in
faith.

Several pastors clearly linked stewardship with grace. Grace is a free gift from God, unmerited:

> You can't buy it; it is given freely. You know, when the retailers announce a half-price sale, we assume that it is not really half-price, that we consumers end up paying somehow. Because nothing is free. But that is not true in religion. Grace is free. Grace makes a person more Christ-like. Giving money is a form of grace and therefore it makes you more Christ-like. That is what the Christian life is all about. There is grace when you see how the money is being used and what good it does. That is a joy in itself. While it's not a "deal with God," when you give you will get grace back.

3.   Money follows ministry. If people are not well served by what the church offers, they are not likely to be generous in their giving.

> People vote two ways in a church, with their feet and with their pocketbook. So if they're giving and coming, we're scratching where it itches somewhere. And if they stop showing up and stop putting money in the plate, then we're failing. You can come up with all these programs and visit everybody's house with a card and have a stewardship committee and say, "What can we count on you, Sister Jones, to give this year?" But if we're not scratching where Brother and Sister Jones are living, and we're not providing a ministry to their youth and to their children, and if they don't feel fed on Sunday morning and feel that people care about them and feel spiritually empowered, that card is not going to make them give.

This pastor represents many, generally from an evangelical orientation, who believe that stewardship programs are unnecessary "if the pastor is doing his job," that is, is providing ministries that serve the people. An evangelical pastor:

> I think that in our church we really touch people so that their faith is central to their lives. If you talk to people who come to this church, they're going to talk in very personal, subjective, pietistic terms about a relationship with Jesus. And when they talk about that, they

mean they're trusting the Lord for their finances, and they believe that what they have, God has put in their hands and they are honoring him with that.

Several pastors with a stewardship orientation told us that the ministries carried out by their churches have strong motivating power. They pointed to the array of ministries in their congregations as evidence of "what God is doing in our midst," for which members should give thanks through pledges and proportionate giving. In the words of one pastor, "the divorce recovery workshop, the growing through grief seminars, the engaged couples class—these and many others are examples of how our church is reaching beyond its own membership in ministering to the whole community."

4. The generations differ. One pastor described the pre-baby boom generation as "achievers" who "tend to give to an ideal or a program." They could be counted on to support the church's work unstintingly. But he was unsure about the new generation coming on:

> I don't know how to term them, maybe "consumers." I think their motivation to join the church is like their motivation to shop in stores. If it offers the product, the baby boomers pay for that project. But the pastor has to make that connection. And somehow we have to find a way of reaching them because we haven't been reaching them with whatever motivational techniques we've been using. As the older folks move on, we've got to replace that giving. We have to make the connection that there is a cost to what they are receiving. I have a theory that churches in the 1960s and 1970s had a real emphasis on youth—retreats, camps, trips, all that kind of stuff was provided. Their parents underwrote that. The parents gave to missions, churches, and to all these programs. The kids, though, were never taught that their parents bring that envelope every Sunday, not taught to give and to make that a part of their lives. They were part of that generation to which everything was given.
>   Now they are grown up, they are bringing their children to receive the same programs, but they still haven't made the connection that somebody has to pay for it. Now they are the income-producing adults who still come to church thinking everything will be paid for.

Somebody has to say: "Wait a minute, what role do *you* play in supporting all this?" So that's what pledging is all about.

Pastors experienced in stewardship campaigns varied in their views of how exclusive an annual stewardship program should be. Should other special appeals be made in addition? How about a separate annual appeal for missions? Ought major needs such as repairing a roof be met solely through Sunday plate offerings or through special appeals? What about major capital projects, such as a new wing or chapel? "Purists" among stewardship pastors maintain that once giving by members is elevated through adoption of true stewardship practice (involving pledging and proportionate giving), no additional raising is necessary. Others disagree, claiming that while this approach may be valid in the longer run, immediate short-run needs cannot really be handled without targeted fund drives. They argue that it matters little whether giving is for one appeal or for multiple appeals. Our own impression is that most successful stewardship pastors allow one or two special appeals yearly, and also that special appeals during the year cause no reduction in stewardship giving.

Perspectives of Lay Members

In our discussions lay members provided unique viewpoints. Laity can evaluate leadership from a certain distance. Three points came up which are worth noting.

1.   Laity need strong support from leaders. Earlier we noted the importance of volunteers in stewardship efforts. Laity were unanimous in praising the kind of support they received as volunteers from pastors, in some cases also appreciating that their pastors felt no need to control everything. Lay volunteers felt affirmed when they were trusted by their pastors and when the pastors conveyed faith that they could do the job. A typical comment: "He keeps us forward-looking and always encourages us." Our pastor "is committed to the Lord and stirs that same commitment in us." Committed laypersons appreciated enthusiasm, clarity, and accountability from staff leaders.

2.   Laypersons voiced varied motivations for giving, illustrating an
important point made by some pastors and stewardship chairpersons:
relatively few parishioners seem truly to internalize the basic theological
theme that we ought to return everything to God because all we have
comes from God.

A married couple exemplifies the different motivations:

WIFE: John and I give to God because everything we have comes from
him in the first place. Our church is a vehicle through which we can
spread the Gospel. It does all the things we think should be done.
HUSBAND: I look at this a little differently. I give to the church, thinking
of the programs that will be benefited. So I don't necessarily think of
giving to God. I also think that consciously we're giving to the church
rather than the government so it's important to realize that giving *is* a
tax advantage. There are so many causes to give to, and we have to
make some tough decisions, even about giving to secular agencies.

In the same vein, a church member for many decades remarked how
little the autumn stewardship campaign said about the church's own
needs:

Rather the campaign says, "Look what you've been a part of this
past year. Here's what your church has been doing through its ministries." As a result you feel you've been investing in something
worthwhile and want to continue your pledging into next year.

His church publishes a church news bulletin mailed to arrive at each
home on Friday or Saturday. It contains, along with Sunday's sermon
topic, catchy photo essays of ministries or missions the church supports,
and it clearly conveys what the church is doing with its money. The
message: "This church is benefiting many in our community and else-
where. It is eminently worth supporting." For many church members this
is a major motivation to support a stewardship campaign.

As one pastor remarked:

A few of the spiritually elite in the church really get that message
and live it fully. They're the ones we ask to witness during our fall

stewardship campaign. But I'd have to say most people are moved to give by our ministries—what they see and are told our church is doing out in the community and beyond.

3.   Numerous laypersons told of the importance of reciprocity with God, particularly members of churches that stress tithing or some version of proportionate giving. A young college student in southern California:

STUDENT: I have heard so many stories of "Wow, God really blessed me because I tithed."
INTERVIEWER: What do you get back out of tithing?
STUDENT: I don't really look to get back, but what I do receive is more than just monetary benefits or whatever. You know, as if I give ten, you will give me twenty for it—that is not how it works. But I can see it in small ways, like I don't have lunch money, and what am I going to do? And it never fails. Someone says, "Oh, let me take you out to lunch." God provides in ways like that.

A Marine sergeant in the West reflected on his family's giving experiences:

The rewards of giving, you just can't explain them. God does bless you and from that, we have given above and beyond our tithes as needs arise. It's weird because I feel that everything I own is not mine, it's God's. I make pretty good money in the military right now so I can help out a little bit more than if I worked a civilian job. A lady lost her father this week. So we went and got groceries for her and made up some meals to send to her today. And then there's a young military couple that just arrived on base. We had some extra furniture so we gave it to them. You know, there's no question about these things.

These people trust God. They have a conviction that once you incorporate giving into your life, a reciprocal relation of trust has been established. God will not let you down. You will not be deprived but rather blessed and cared for in ways you do not expect and that transcend rational calculation.

In sum, the theology of stewardship is deemed capable of producing a radical transformation in how individuals regard their money, time, and talents. When a person understands the stewardship ideal, we were told, the result is tantamount to a conversion experience. This is stewardship at its purest, and nobody should confuse it with a fund-raising technique or a four-week program in the fall. We must realize that it doesn't succeed for every member. Some are saints and many others are not. The pastors and stewardship staff we met knew this in their bones and stood ready with other forms of appeals.

We also need to reiterate the importance of participation and ownership. In successful stewardship churches, lay members expected to share decision making in virtually every aspect of the program. They had a sense of ownership. Laity, when openly invited by the pastor to share their ideas about the program and when taken seriously, gain a sense of being involved in an important collective endeavor. As their sense of ownership grows, their willingness to contribute does too. This requires that the leaders are secure enough to forego a need to control everything and willing to create a truly cooperative endeavor. The results of the best collaborative stewardship programs we saw were truly transformative for all.

For Reflection and Discussion

1. How do you define "stewardship"? How do you distinguish between stewardship and fund raising?

2. What is the central theological principle of stewardship as you understand it?

3. Look at the five characteristics of a successful stewardship strategy (p. 81). Which of these characteristics are present in your congre-gation? How could missing or weak characteristics be provided or strengthened in your congregation?

4. Do you agree or disagree with the following statements? Why?

• Stewardship depends on vision.
• Stewardship education takes time and planning.

- A sound theology of stewardship encourages giving out of thank-fulness and a vision that everything we have comes from God.
- Money follows ministry.
- Members of different generations have different motivations and styles for giving.

CHAPTER 6

Stewardship Issues: Pledging, Tithing, and Budgets

Building a strong stewardship church is not a casual undertaking. Experienced stewardship pastors made that clear. Church members must be challenged to consider higher levels of giving than they have been used to. The pastor must establish pledging, and must ask parishioners to consider raising their giving by a percentage point or two. He or she may also hold up tithing as an ideal, whether a full tithe to the church, or "half a tithe" with a suggestion to give another half to community charities.

In this chapter we listen to pastors reflect on pledging, tithing, and related issues: full disclosure of finances, "faith giving," the pastor's own giving, how pastors compare evangelical churches in these respects with their own churches, and how to integrate the budget into a stewardship approach.

Pledging

Our earlier research confirmed that church members who make annual pledges clearly give more money. Members who attend church regularly tend more often to pledge, and members of larger churches tend more often to pledge (except in the Assemblies of God). Presbyterian congregations lead the five denominations in the frequency of using pledge cards, followed in order by Lutheran, Catholic, Assemblies of God, and Southern Baptist congregations. Seventy-eight percent of Presbyterian church members approve of pledge cards, compared with 58 percent of Lutherans, 48 percent of Catholics, 41 percent of Southern Baptists, and

37 percent of Assembly of God members. Beyond these statistics lie four issues that concern pastors.

1.   Members have different motivations for pledging.

Pastors imbued with a stewardship ideal say to the people, as one Episcopalian rector put it, "Let's give out of thankfulness, out of that covenant relationship with God, in response to what God has done for us." But he admitted that many lay leaders see pledging differently, as support for programs:

> What lay leaders say to the people is, "You've got to give more because we've got to get a better program going here." I think that is one of the biggest motivations for why people really give here. They want to see that they are giving to a program they like. And if the money isn't being used for programs they like, they let us know. . . . My response is that if we would just be generous and give out of gratitude like we should, then we wouldn't fight over programs and you wouldn't hear, "We don't do enough here for this, or this." We would be able to do it all.

Pastors frequently noted this difference in perspective: from the pastor come stewardship themes of giving out of thankfulness, but typical lay members are more moved to pledge by what they see the church doing with their money, both outward ministry like a shelter for the homeless and programs of personal and family growth for the parishioners, such as Bible study, Sunday school classes for children, youth programs, and divorce recovery workshops. Pastors often try to combine the two by linking thankfulness to ministry: "Look at what God is doing through our church. Should we not thank God generously by continuing to support God's gifts we see all around us?" Many pastors are content with that de facto division of labor, that the pastor lays the biblical and theological foundations for generous giving while lay members of the stewardship committee point to the necessity of supporting programs.

2.   How much should people be asked to pledge?

Most mainline pastors advocate some kind of proportionate giving in stewardship sermons. Tithing is often mentioned as a kind of yardstick.

The Assemblies of God is an example of a full tithing denomination, in other words, membership carries with it an expectation that you will tithe 10 percent of your gross income to the church. Membership in a mainline church does not carry this expectation. Presbyterian and Lutheran congregations in our study were most likely to report that tithing is an ideal but not obligatory, or that giving a proportion of one's income, but not tithing, is emphasized. Most pastors acknowledge other calls on their members' generosity. For example:

PASTOR: We've been pushing tithing here for about eight or ten years now. We let you [parishioners] define tithing. We say that tithing is based on the 10 percent figure in the Bible. It's a form of proportionate giving. Now some of our folks give to other charities. So we say, "Why don't you consider that you tithe to charities in general and we'd like you to consider giving half of that to your church. So 5 percent would be a tithe here." And some say they will give 5 percent of their net income because the government takes the rest, and some of that money goes for charity, too, and for running the government and for public order. So we let people define what they mean when they say they tithe. We have a young woman in our church who is very vocal, a leader in this church in tithing and in strong stewardship. She'll get up in church and say, "My grandmother taught me that when I receive my paycheck, I sit down and I write 10 percent to the church."
INTERVIEWER: Isn't she unusual?
PASTOR: Well, there are more people now who are using the tithing language than when I came to this church. So we're making progress on it. And I think it's a legitimate way because it's the whole proportionate giving model. What's discouraging is to know how many millionaires you have in your church and to realize that they're not giving anything that comes close to a proportion of their income.

Other pastors prefer to back off of talk about full tithing, but still to challenge their members. A Lutheran pastor:

I preach more percentage giving than tithing. It's a dash of cold water to say to somebody that they must go from a life of self-centered spending to a 10 percent tithe. I think it's not realistic, and it's not pastoral. I believe the people have to receive both the law and the joy of the Gospel. The law may be the tithe, but the joy is reaching a goal that one has set for one's spiritual growth. So I preach percentage giving. I preach it relentlessly.

Most pastors say they have no idea what proportion of their membership tithes. In one large Presbyterian church, the pastor preaches tithing, but, like the Lutheran pastor above, does not insist on it. He will only say that the secret of his church's large revenues is that "we have a large number of people giving, and many give at a high rate considering their capacity."

When a church engages in every member canvassing, should any number be suggested, even indirectly, about how much a family or an individual might pledge, based on the occupations of the adults? This approach, favored by a consultant hired by one church, resulted in disaster. Members responded to the canvassers with anger and alienation ("How dare you . . . ?"). The next year the church adopted a "faith pledge" system advocated by the denomination. On pledge Sunday, two separate baskets were brought forward. One contained cards with only pledge amounts written on them, and the other contained only cards with the names of persons pledging. But no names could be associated with specific pledges. Church members we interviewed liked this practice, saying they felt greatly at ease knowing that no one knew what anyone pledged.

3.   Some people resist pledging.

Clergy described how some parishioners can be hesitant. A Baptist pastor:

> The arguments I have encountered against pledging are first that you should not ask people to make a promise; it is between the individual and the Lord, and if you make a promise, somehow that invalidates it. I guess then you are giving for more legalistic reasons than for internally motivated reasons. I suppose it makes it more of a transaction and maybe less spontaneous. And the other argument is that some people feel like they don't know what their income will be. We then point out that people make a promise when they sign a mortgage or when they buy a car with monthly payments or use a credit card!

From another pastor:

When people look at the amount they give to the church, they are embarrassed. When people are asked, "If the Lord is really the Lord of your life, can somebody tell that by your check stubs?" they're embarrassed. They don't want to face it.

Further hesitation comes from recent economic downturns and layoffs. People are concerned, as one pastor put it, with "those big 'what ifs.' It's hard for them to pledge if they're uncertain, and particularly if they have children at home." Virtually all pastors we talked to insisted that they tell church members they can always renegotiate a pledge, or even let it drop, if they find themselves in economic straits.

In a word, pledging (including tithing where it is preached) seems least offensive to parishioners when encased in stewardship preaching and teaching. A pledge or tithe then undergoes a kind of transformation. It becomes an occasion to consider in a concrete way what I or we should return to God for all God has done for me, for us, for our family, for our church. In a strong stewardship church, such as one Presbyterian church we visited, giving is spiritualized. Prayer groups form during the fall stewardship season to pray explicitly for success of the stewardship drive. A yearly motto is devised by the pastor and stewardship committee, such as "We're Here for Life," and appears as a logo on all stewardship mailings and handouts. On the two pledging Sundays, a reverent procession with choir accompaniment brings forward the pledges to be offered at the service. Thus giving becomes sacralized rather than a secular question of "How much are we supposed to come up with?" and pledging is inseparable from the spiritual sense of mission.

4.   Acknowledging pledges is a high priority with some pastors.

For example, a Lutheran:

My model is to acknowledge every pledge—every pledge!—with a personal note. I mention the amount of the pledge. This does two things. It gets out the word in the neighborhood that "the pastor wrote me a note about my pledge. I only pledged five dollars a

week, but he wrote me a note!" And what I say in that note is,
"You've made a great first step, bless your soul! The first thing in
good stewardship is setting a goal. And when you find joy in it,
you'll want to give and give and give. I'm celebrating that with
you. We think that's a great gift. There's room to grow." Nobody's
going to be offended by that.

Three other general topics came up relating to stewardship.

Are Evangelical Churches Better at Stewardship?

Many pastors believe that evangelical churches have a leg up over mainline churches when it comes to stewardship. Mainline churches, in the
view of a Presbyterian consultant, "have substituted something called
'church membership' for discipleship. And membership has a static
quality about it: The church is an institution you join and support and
you attend when you want to, and you support it and keep it going. And
you don't have any great expectation that you are going to grow or
change significantly. It's like membership in a club."

A Lutheran pastor:

Evangelical congregations have a higher intensity of religious experience . . . a level of expected commitment that is a step above
the mainline. The community has a higher intensity of commitment
and therefore gives more. And the mainline churches have constantly been tempted to settle for less. I think we can close the gap. But
it requires a higher intensity and demand and challenge than some
people are willing to accept.

Other pastors urge caution in praising evangelical churches too un-
critically. A veteran Lutheran pastor, while admitting that evangelical
churches "ask biblically and believe biblically a lot more than we do,"
expressed his discomfort with "the reward thing and the law thing" that
for him are part of evangelical attitudes toward money. A United
Church of Christ pastor compared his liberal denomination with evangelicals in level of commitment:

Part of our problem is that we do not call our people to commitment. The Gospel doesn't ask for ten minutes on Sunday, it asks for your entire life. Now, I think you can be an ultraliberal and give your whole life. I'm not sure a conservative theology has anything to do with commitment. That has to do with how I read the Gospel. *Sojourners* is a magazine I really enjoy—a solid, evangelical, almost fundamentalist, ultraliberal magazine—because the commitment calls for social justice. I'm not going to say the Assemblies of God approach is wrong. It doesn't speak to me, but it's not wrong. It's one of their gifts and I need to hear them because they challenge me. And they need to hear me because I challenge them. But God isn't calling me to any less commitment than he calls them. As long as the UCC waters down that call, we're going to have watered-down commitment.

Full Disclosure of Finances

There was strong consensus among the pastors we talked to in favor of financial openness. One pastor advocated full discussion of finances in a stewardship drive. He resisted the idea of faith giving—an emphasis that downplays financial data:

I think that all giving is giving in faith. I'm a guy who was brought up among New York parishioners and Greenwich people who worked on Wall Street. They like to see the figures and like to know where their money's going. I don't think there's anything disgraceful about knowing where one's money is going. In fact, I think it's responsible! I like to know, when I give, where my money is going. I don't want to give my money to a situation under faith giving and find out that it ends up supporting these ultraright groups. I think there's nothing unfaithful about that. . . . I think every taxpayer in America might want to know where his or her money goes. Why shouldn't church people be in the same boat? The material we pass out in a stewardship drive in our church spells out where the money is going and why it is going there; if there is an increase, why.

Full financial disclosure includes disclosing the pastor's salary. This causes nervousness for some. Many mainline denominations require public disclosure of pastors' salaries, but not all. An Episcopal pastor:

> Leading the fall stewardship campaign was often uncomfortable for me. I was aware that I was asking people to contribute to my salary, which was usually the biggest item in the budget. Emotionally the bind had to do with asking people to pledge to God, but knowing that it was coming to me. [1]

A parishioner we interviewed was even more explicit. After praising the pastor and acknowledging that the parish was "extraordinarily lucky to have him," she continued:

> I think our biggest problem is, and we've heard it over and over again recently, the high level of his salary as a result of his being in this parish eighteen years. And he's also the senior full-time clergy member in the diocese. So on the projected salary scale, his salary is very high. In fact, he earns more money than anybody in public life, typically here the superintendent of schools or the local hospital administrator. Those are benchmark figures coming from a community's sense of what the top-paying public job should be. He went past that a few years ago, and it has created an unease among many parishioners.

The vestry (lay council) in an Episcopal church must approve a pastor's salary, but they deliberate in relation to salary guidelines set down by the diocese. In other denominations, setting the pastor's salary is largely at the discretion of the congregation. Regardless of the process, this salary is often among the biggest budget items, and full disclosure may not eliminate a sense of unease felt both by the pastor and by church members who are otherwise strongly supportive. Full disclosure alleviates the problem but does not remove it.

The Budget and Faith Giving

Should the budget be formulated prior to a stewardship campaign and displayed centrally in the campaign? If this is done, the campaign becomes budget-driven and is pitched toward meeting the budget. Or should the campaign emphasize stewardship theology and giving out of thankfulness, while keeping budget figures hidden? The latter is called "faith giving." We listened to advocates of both. A Lutheran pastor told us that a budget and full financial disclosure are imperative:

PASTOR: We think a fall stewardship program is a time for accountability to the parishioner. It says "Here's what we have been doing." So part of our message is an inventory of the growing programs and services this congregation provides. Next, we share what we'd like to do with the money we're asking members to pledge for next year. If we had X thousand more dollars, here's how we would spend it. Finally, we point out that we can't pay for all of the services we provide. So we need volunteers, and here's an up-to-date list of the kinds of volunteer services we need.

INTERVIEWER: But one approach is "faith giving." It says you shouldn't talk about the budget, but rather about the life of stewardship and accountability.

PASTOR: I don't get excited about this and I never have because most of the people I've known in my lifetime don't think well in the abstract. They think in specifics and there's nothing more specific in human experience than dollars and cents as a measure of value, commitment, vision, and faith. So faith giving may be wonderful in certain kinds of cultural settings, but for Pennsylvania Dutchmen, for government employees here, for corporate executives in Pittsburgh, for working folks in Baltimore, where I've been, I've never seen people who thought that way. They thought in concrete where the rubber hits the road. . . . It doesn't fit the people I've worked with.

The opposite strategy, employed by many stewardship pastors, is to downplay the budget in favor of an emphasis on giving as part of the spiritual life. A Lutheran stewardship officer:

I recommend that you sever the budget process from the response process, that you hold up the ministries of the church and what you're doing to meet human needs as the motivation. A budget does not motivate people; it just gets them anxious. Budgets should not be goals to be reached because that is limiting. "If we meet our budget, we've done it." But to be the steward means that we need to strive as persons to prioritize whatever time, money, and energy we have, not in serving self but in serving others. So to hold up those teachings about being a steward is critical.

In this approach members are asked to focus not on meeting church needs or ministries, but instead on what they themselves need to give as a measure of trust and sacrifice and a response to God's love. After the pledges are totaled up the budget-setting process should begin. One veteran pastor, in discussing this issue, asked a central question: "Aren't we supposed to be in the disciple-making business?" His point of view was notable:

PASTOR: What I find is that many pastors start at the wrong end. They've got a bunch of nominal Christians, half-hearted disciples, so they keep trying to either find clever new gimmicks or they try to beat the half-hearted disciples over the head to give more generously. It seems to me the heart of the problem is, how do you move them to become mature disciples? And if they become mature disciples, you probably won't have to beat them over the head to give generously. I think that's the heart of the issue. Stewardship is a byproduct of discipleship.
INTERVIEWER: What does that mean in reality for the pastor?
PASTOR: It means that you're really trying to help people grow as Christians, trying to help them grow in the faith, in their understanding, in their involvement. My experience is that when people grow in their discipleship, their stewardship comes along.

The pastors and churches we studied were split on this issue of budget-centered giving versus faith giving. All generally agreed that faith giving is closer to the theological ideal, but pastors talked to us about what worked best for them in their churches in the past, and this influenced their approach now. All were cautious and pragmatic. They came to different conclusions on the issue, and their actual practices varied.

This issue of budget appeals versus faith giving is a variation on the central issue of church finances—fund raising versus stewardship. It is a matter of faith.

For Reflection and Discussion

1. Do members of your congregation pledge? Why or why not? If you wanted to encourage people to change their practice (to begin pledging or to stop pledging), what two or three arguments would you present?

2. What are your views on the issues related to pledging outlined in the chapter: motivating members to pledge (p. 96), who should see pledges, how much people should be asked to pledge (p. 96), acknowledging pledges (p. 99)?

3. Do you think evangelical churches are better at stewardship? Why or why not? If you think they are better, what do you think mainline congregations could learn from them?

4. What does "full disclosure" mean to you? Do you think it is a generally helpful or unhelpful practice? Why?

CHAPTER 7

Church Invested Funds

Church invested reserve funds are on the rise in all denominations and especially in mainline Protestantism. Reserve funds include endowments, but they also include other funds that the church has set aside and invested. Here we are discussing what are commonly called "endowments," broadly understood.

In our 1993 survey, we asked how many churches had endowments, and we found that the proportion with endowments of $100,000 or more was 1 percent in the Assemblies of God, 3 percent in the Southern Baptist Convention, 10 percent in the Catholic Church, 12 percent in the Evangelical Lutheran Church in America, and 18 percent in the Presbyterian Church (U.S.A.). These figures may not be precise, but they portray the situation in general.

Widespread discussion about endowments and church reserve funds is new. Historically, endowments were commonly rejected by evangelical churches as theologically indefensible. Why store up wealth when there are sinners to be saved and hungry people to be fed *now*? But the topic of reserve funds has been brought up again in recent years. Catholics did not discuss them in the past because little investment money was available. But it is now. Hence reserve funds are a new issue in many religious groups.

Presbyterian churches with an endowment have formed an association called the National Association of Endowed Presbyterian Churches, and the Episcopalian churches with endowments have formed a similar group. The Presbyterian group carried out a survey of endowed churches in 1995 that provides some of the most reliable information available today.[1]

The Presbyterian association estimated that about 500 to 600

Presbyterian churches (out of a total of 11,400 nationwide) possess endowments of $500,000 or more. About 100 churches have funds of $2.5 million or more. The survey found that church endowments are usually in multiple and diverse funds. Seldom does a church have a single unified endowment fund; typically the money has come in through various bequests that are managed as separate funds today. Also it is common that churches do not call these funds "endowments," which implies that only the interest income, not the principal, can be spent. Some churches avoid the term entirely, and in other churches the lay members are not fully aware of their church's reserve funds.

By all accounts, the size of church reserves is growing year by year. The past half century of American life has been a time of financial well-being, and many church members have built up family fortunes. *Fortune* magazine cites estimates that Americans over age sixty have accumulated $7 trillion in net worth, which will form the basis for their bequests as they die.[2] *Fortune* calls this the largest transfer of wealth in United States history.

Reports from experts today indicate that the greatest beneficiaries of the American transfer of wealth are colleges and universities. Health-related organizations are in second place. Churches are behind. Yet clearly the flow of money to churches is rising. For example, Larry Carr, president of the Presbyterian Church (U.S.A.) Foundation, said that whereas in 1982 Presbyterian churches received bequests of $25 million, by 1995 the figure had grown to $75 million. In Carr's words: "We are on a geometric curve with the amount of dollars coming to Presbyterian churches . . . . In our most guarded estimates, we wouldn't be surprised if the amount of dollars coming to Presbyterian causes exceeds 20 billion dollars over the next 20 years."[3] Other denominations report similar trends. Reserves are growing everywhere.

Investments Dependency

An important piece of information is the amount of dependence a church has on invested funds for its annual budget. "Investments dependency" is defined as the percentage of the current budget that comes from income on investments. If a church's annual budget is $200,000 and its income from investments supporting the budget is $20,000, its investments dependency is 10 percent.

In the 1995 survey of endowed Presbyterian churches, some were as high as 80 percent investments dependent. But this was the exception. More commonly a church was 10, 20, or 30 percent investments dependent. The average was 26 percent, and the median was 21 percent. (The lower median figure than average here indicates that many churches have a low dependency figure and only a few have a high figure—but a few have a *much* higher figure.)

Investments dependency is a function of the size of the reserves, the size of the budget, and the extent to which investment income is used to support the budget. A church whose reserves are constituted such that most of the income cannot be used for ongoing expenses will have a low investments dependency. This situation is widespread in Presbyterian churches, as for example when a donor specifies that the income can be used only for missions, only for seminary expenses of ministerial students, or only for upkeep of the building, grounds, or the organ. We believe that in general, church life is less affected by reserves in churches that are less investments dependent for their ongoing program. A church's investments dependency is all-important to the effects of its reserves on church life.

The pastors we interviewed were aware of the dangers of allowing investments dependency to get too high. One pastor told of one of his previous congregations that had both a sizable endowment and a large operating budget of $900,000. That congregation decided that it would restrict itself to using only $300,000 in endowment income each year to support the budget (producing an investments dependency of one-third), although it could have drawn more. He approved, but he thought that even this was too high. In his opinion, investments dependency should not exceed 20 percent.

A Presbyterian pastor summed up the dangers of a high investments dependency:

> I think the use of investments is harmful only if it goes to the extreme. There are churches from which some wealthy families have moved, but the wealth has stayed. On any given Sunday morning there are a dozen people there, yet the building is gorgeous, they pay a preacher, they pay a person to make music, but they really have no substantial life.

Several other issues were addressed in the Presbyterian endowment survey. One is how the funds are invested. In these churches, an average of 43 percent of the assets were invested in bonds, 42 percent were in stocks, 10 percent were in money markets or certificates of deposit, 2 percent were in real estate, and 2 percent were in other places. Average income in the previous year was 6.1 percent of the principal. Sixty-five percent of the churches have a written policy concerning the use of income from the funds. Twenty-four percent have a written policy concerning socially responsible investment of the funds. Eighty-seven percent reported regularly to the congregation on the total amount of the endowment principal, and 94 percent reported regularly to the congregation on the total amount of endowment income. In most churches the reporting to members on the state of invested funds and income has improved in the last few years.

Church leaders have strong feelings for and against church invested funds, and we heard all kinds of viewpoints. Here we will list the principal arguments for and against.

Arguments for Invested Funds

We heard a variety of arguments in support of invested funds. The first is practical. It states that some church members are inclined to give to an endowment fund whereas they would not give to annual budgets or to other funds. Therefore having an endowment increases overall giving. It seems that some donors take the long view and desire that their gift serve the church for decades to come. There is something appealing about a donation to a church that will remain in perpetuity and that will bear an eternal name memorializing the donor, such as "The Thompson Bequest" or "The McIntosh Fund."

A Presbyterian pastor told us:

There are some people who give very sparingly during their lifetime, for fear, perhaps, that if they give away too much they are not going to have anything left for their old age. Somehow they make it through their lives, and somehow they have money left over. Then they give money to the church that perhaps they should have been giving all these years. Well, why not use that money for the benefit of the church? I accept using money from the past to help the present, just as money from the present is building for the future.

Pastors often emphasize the long term. Life is short, and history is long. Sermons remind members that "you can't take it with you" and we should consider the kind of world we would like for future generations. As a part of their stewardship message pastors should be helping church members to think about what they want to support in the future. Giving to an endowment promotes the values donors cherish long after they die. For these reasons, the argument goes, churches need to have endowments in place to receive such long-term gifts.

A second argument is that churches by their very nature depend for their survival on wealth stored over many years and expended gradually. This is normal. It is proper, proponents say, that church members with excess wealth will put some into long-term endowments, and the churches themselves will set aside some savings because churches need these storehouses of wealth to carry them over lean times. Wealth is stored for eternity to do good for eternity.

Writers who predict lean years for American Protestantism in the early twenty-first century make this argument. They say that the decades ahead will see lower religious giving, so today we need to store up wealth from the high level of giving.[3] It is the same principle as saving up during seven fat years to carry us over the seven lean years ahead. It is simple, honest prudence.

A third argument is related to the second. The value of reserves is not just that they purchase future survival; they also provide for vitality and effectiveness at all times. Having reserves gives a church stability, self-confidence, and increased freedom of action. Reserves allow churches to be innovative in pursuing mission and ministry opportunities. The churches can take risks and undertake new initiatives. For instance, an Episcopal rector recalled an urban church where she had previously served as an assistant. At one time it had been the largest church in the diocese, but had since fallen on difficult times as the neighborhood had changed. An endowment was crucial to its revitalization.

It's so clear to me that that church needs to be there. They have a flourishing ministry with homeless people, a ministry for people with AIDS. The neighborhood would have been impoverished; the city would have been impoverished, without that church's presence.

As it turns out, they now have a new rector and those leaner times are now behind them, and they're reclaiming a much bigger presence and a much bigger sense of who they are and what they can do, how they can reach out, how they can minister, and how they can witness.

Maybe some churches need to be closed because they're just museum pieces, but I think a lot of urban churches that now are just subsisting on the interest from their investments are rediscovering who they can be now in very changed circumstances.

A fourth argument is closely related to the third. Investment income from reserves encourages congregation-wide discussions about how best to use the money. These discussions are energizing to all the people. Do the church's priorities lie with merely meeting the budget and expanding the program? What *is* the most important thing? Churches with reserves can see farther, and they can be an example to others.

One instance of being an example arises on the topic of where to invest the funds. Several pastors told us that their congregations had agreed on a lower rate of return on some reserves by investing them in social action causes, for example, nonprofit organizations that use the funds to refurbish homes in decaying neighborhoods. Investments of this type allow the congregation to do a meaningful project while still earning a small return. Actions such as this inspire members and sometimes even inspire other churches.

Finally, one pastor observed that church endowments and other reserves are just one kind of wealth that a congregation inherits from previous generations. She pointed out that the buildings, grounds, and organ are also inherited, and she wondered why reserve accounts should be viewed differently from these. On a theological level, if one accepts that "all good things come from God," then a church has an obligation to be a steward of financial assets as well as its physical assets.

Arguments against Church Invested Funds

Arguments we have heard against church invested funds can be grouped into five types. The first and most common says that a church with large reserves will become lazy in giving because it can survive very well on investment income. In other words, reserves hurt annual giving. The logic of the argument is simple, but the empirical reality is more complex. Let us explain.

We have heard numerous speakers give examples of churches with large invested reserves whose giving was low because they did not feel the need to promote high annual giving by members, and we do not doubt the stories. But individual cases and individual stories cannot test the theory; only controlled data gathering and analysis can do that. When this is done, the finding is always that churches with large invested reserves in general do not have lower giving. This was the result in our 1993 five-denomination study. Even when we controlled all other relevant variables we had the same outcome: if all else is constant, giving to endowed and nonendowed churches is the same. (We had no way to test the influence of investments dependency on giving.) The same was also found in the 1995 survey of endowed Presbyterian churches. To be precise: the size of the endowment had no discernible influence on level of giving, but the investments dependency ratio was related to giving. High-dependency churches had moderately lower per-member giving than low-dependency churches.[4]

How can we explain these findings? Isn't it logical that members of churches with invested reserves will feel less urgency to give? Our best guess is that having investments in and of itself has no definite impact on per-member giving, but a high investments dependency has a depressing effect. The investments dependency of most churches is too low to introduce complacency about annual stewardship. Having a dependency of 10 or 20 percent is not enough to lull the stewardship activity to sleep or to convince members that they do not need to give. An additional reason is that some church reserve accounts are set up to disallow any large flow of funds from investment income to the general budget. When this is the case, the investments dependency cannot rise very high regardless of the size of the reserves.

In their survey of pastors, John and Sylvia Ronsvalle asked if the existence of endowments discouraged contributions. Their respondents were split down the middle, with 40 percent agreeing that endowments do discourage giving, 38 percent expressing the belief that they do not, and the rest undecided.[5] The pastors we interviewed tended to believe that reserves do depress giving. A United Methodist pastor reflected the views of many:

> I guess I just have a lack of faith. I feel that if indeed we were to empty out our coffers overnight and spend that money for mission and operate on a budget of "what we have is what we spend," no, I don't think that we would have the level necessary to keep up with the programs we have. Other people—people on the other side of the fence—would say that this shows a lack of faith, and that indeed the money would come in.

Several pastors told us that the tendency toward lower giving because of invested reserves could be mitigated if the proper stewardship message is preached. A Presbyterian pastor:

> Well, people say that if a church has reserves, the members will think the church is rich and they don't have to give. So you have to run a stewardship program that says you're not giving to the church's budget. You're giving out of response to what the Lord has done. And the more we can receive in the church, the more we can do. You have to give the people a vision. If people are just giving to the church budget, reserves will hurt you. But if people have a vision, investment income won't hurt.

The researchers carrying out the Presbyterian survey interviewed numerous people and found that all had heard the argument that endowments depress giving. Most did not know if the argument was true or false, and some asked for research to clarify the question. Several told of test situations that might provide clues, for example, when a church received a large bequest and then charted giving by the membership in the following few years to see if it went down or not. In the interviews many church leaders seemed to believe that a high investments dependency is a bad thing for a church, and they hoped to reduce the level of dependency in their own churches.[6] We find this convincing.

A second argument asserts that any excess wealth in a church should be spent for mission now, not stored up for institutional expenses in the future. This argument has two elements: (a) spending versus saving wealth for the future, and (b) spending for mission versus spending for the institution. The issues are separable, but often the two are voiced together. The debate arises from the view of some Protestants that church institutions should not become too wealthy, too established, or too prideful. Rather, they should spend their excess wealth to do God's will in the world now. Wealth is to be used, not just collected. In their view, Christian churches should travel light and trust the Lord for their future survival. Each generation needs to pay its own bills. Some churches even have definite policies that any large gift from a member must be expended within a definite period of time, for example, three years, and it should be used to enhance overall Christian mission.

A variation on this argument is that congregations should forward all (or at least a large proportion) of the contributions that they receive for endowment on to the larger church. Similar reasoning applies: rather than allowing itself to accumulate wealth, the congregation should send these funds to the denomination, whose leaders see the bigger picture and can allocate funds to missions, church development, or other areas where they are needed most. One pastor recalled a situation where a large multinational organization, looking to expand its headquarters building, wanted to purchase the property of a Presbyterian church.

> They offered the church $10 million to move. The church took the money and built on a different lot. It didn't cost them $10 million to build the new church. The church is done now, and it's very well appointed! But some people thought it was an abomination. They said that they should have taken the $10 million and given it to the presbytery for endowment and for the starting of new churches, and I would have bought that view.

That same minister formerly pastored a church that had a policy of forwarding half of all contributions to endowment to the denomination. The congregation kept only half. He said that not all members liked the idea, but due to his leadership they went along.

An Episcopal pastor, who admitted that his parish relies heavily on investment income for its operating budget, disagreed. He would prefer that the reserves remain at the congregational level.

This is another issue that is really hot right now because across the board, the economy is the same in the church as it is in the nation. Everybody is hurting, and everybody is going down. The national church economy is going down, but the local parish church is going down everywhere. The local church has got to be strong in order for the national church to be strong. I feel that the local church has got to do whatever it can to strengthen itself as it supports the larger church. But it cannot give up itself for the larger church because then, in five years, there will be no more local church. And then the larger church will have no support and it will collapse. The people in the local church, if you gave away their reserves, would be furious. They would say, "You have given away my church!" so we would lose many folks.

A third argument is related to the second and has several facets. Basically it criticizes endowments because they tend to be set up for causes not very central to what Christianity is about. In reality, endowments are most commonly set up in single churches, and sometimes they are for beautification, building maintenance, music programs, and other causes that overemphasize a love for monuments, pride, status, and show. Proponents of this argument are not opposed to endowments in principle, but they are opposed to how endowments are set up in reality. They say that a good endowment would be established to support missions, outreach, education, or social witness; a bad endowment would support institutional maintenance and social status for a very delimited social group. The worst kind of endowment would be established to pay for conspicuous consumption in a single congregation. The result is a kind of idolatry of architecture and group status.

A component of this problem is that large reserves in one church set up tensions between it and the neighboring churches—some of whose pastors are envious and even resentful. We have seen situations in which pastors of churches with large reserves feel they cannot mix with other pastors in the area because of the negativity and sniping that occurs.

Frequently the issue boils down to whether the investment income from the endowments will be restricted or unrestricted. Almost all of the pastors we spoke with favored unrestricted endowments. A Presbyterian pastor reacted sharply when we asked him a hypothetical question about a congregation member who wanted to establish an endowment for church landscaping.

I'd take the matter to the session. But we're not going to turn the
place into Busch Gardens, and put up redwood trees or whatever
just to please him. And if it doesn't fit in with what the church
stands for, then a large garden isn't in the picture.

An Episcopal priest told us of a nearby church:

A person was going to give a huge amount of money, but it had to
be used to put a flagpole and a revolutionary war cannon in front
of the church. This is because the donors were involved in some
revolutionary war group like the DAR or something like that. This
is a horrendous example of how people can use the church by giving
money but stipulating that it be used in a certain way.

His parish has a policy of refusing to accept any restricted gifts, no
matter how worthy the cause.

We are a community of people who have to make decisions about
how we use our money. I feel strongly about that. We need to decide, as a group, what is important in our mission. So if you get
someone who says they will give you a million dollars if only you
will use it for a particular purpose and then name some specific one
of fifty missions that might be important to us, then that person is
running the boat. So we say to folks, "We welcome your money,
we'd love to have your money, but you have got to let the vestry
and the parish decide how the money is going to be used."

A Presbyterian pastor also favored unrestricted over restricted
endowments, but his reasoning differed from that of the other pastors.

I've heard horror stories of universities and churches that have
gotten endowments with a restriction that seemed to make sense
when it was given, but the purpose for which it was given had
disappeared. Forty years later, they still couldn't use the money.
I've been told that you can go to court and break these restrictions.
But that's a problem.

This pastor agreed with the Episcopal priest that the congregation's ruling body should allocate funds, but he would not be as hard-nosed about restricted gifts.

> We encourage people that if they want to give an endowment with a restriction, the session will consider that, and if it's something we think is part of our vision, we'll accept it. Otherwise we turn them down. If you have a vision, you won't let the endowment run you. You can't let the tail wag the dog.

A related problem is how far the congregation is willing to bend its principles in order to accommodate potentially large contributors to endowment. One pastor told us of a member in another church who owned a brewery, and who wanted to use a sizable amount of the brewery's profits to establish an endowment. The pastor declined his offer. But the Presbyterian pastor who told us disagreed with this decision:

> I'll take all the alcohol money I can get, frankly, and put it to good use, if he wants to give it away. I won't give him a dime for his operation. But I'll take his money, sure, and give it to the poor. In our church we had a policy that we wouldn't give to any organization that dehumanized life in any way, shape, or form. But I must be frank with you and say that I am glad to take it. I won't help them make it, but I'll take it.

That pastor would draw the line, though, as he related an experience from the 1960s:

> I have turned down money. During the Vietnam War, I had somebody promise to give the church half a million dollars if I would not mention Vietnam from the pulpit. I told him in graceful terms to go to hell. I informed the session, and some of them looked at me askance and said, "Do you really have to mention Vietnam from the pulpit?" and I said, "Well no, I don't have to. You can get another pastor." But no money was going to coerce me to do anything.

This argument is not opposed to endowments in principle so much as to the way many are being set up. The worst kind is one that benefits elements of institutional life in a church that smell of pride and status rather than generosity and outreach. The best kind supports mission and outreach rather than some element of consumption or show. We agree with the pastors who emphasized that a church needs to have its policies and priorities in order, so that when a gift comes in, the church knows how to respond. Otherwise when a gift comes the church needs to go into a crash program.

A fourth argument is less often heard, and it relates to the psychology of an endowment rather than the endowment itself. It argues that a church with an endowment is released from the necessary discipline of a yearly balanced budget. A church with an endowment can do "deficit financing" by "borrowing" from the endowment principal. Indeed, this occurs in endowed churches, and so the argument is based on real life. It frequently happens that church staff desires an enlarged program or a new capital expenditure and finds a way to "borrow" funds from the endowment principal to do it. They make a promise of some kind to repay the amount borrowed, but in reality the promise is often ignored or reinterpreted later.

Put simply, a church with reserves is not forced to be trim and efficient. In adverse times it can coast along and avoid hard decisions for many years. In the extreme, the very reason for a particular congregation even to exist may have disappeared, yet it lingers on through inertia with investment income support.

This argument is really a caution against human tendencies and practices that creep into churches with reserves. The response to this argument, in our view, is that reserves need to be managed with care and integrity.

A fifth argument is infrequent, although we have heard it. We believe it is less important than the first four. It holds that having reserves inevitably brings a new level of conflict into a church. If there are no reserves, there is no tussle over how to use the investment income. But once a gift comes in and is accepted, the church needs to cope with endless tension over this sore point. This argument is difficult to evaluate. Do reserves in themselves raise the level of conflict? Maybe. We believe the problem, whether large or small, can be reduced through prudence and foresight.

One way to control a conflict over investment income is to avoid setting up committees virtually preordained to take opposite positions on the spend-versus-save continuum. Churches should avoid putting the spenders (like ambitious staff) in one committee and the savers (like conservative trustees) in another. And if this happens anyway, make sure communication is open at all times. We have observed churches trying various committee structures, including unicameral or bicameral governance, to constrain problems of tension between committees. Suspicion that the managers of the investments are not forthright and truthful can easily grow in some circles of church members. Perhaps the best solution is for the congregation to establish guidelines up front about how investment income is to be managed. The clearer the policy, the less is the likelihood of controversy erupting.

Two topics seem to cause conflict. One is accountability, and the other is social responsibility in investing. On accountability, the pastors we interviewed were resolute in affirming its importance.

A Presbyterian pastor:

Whenever the gift is given, there must be accountability so it doesn't go down somebody's particular drain. If I were to give $10 million to the church, I'd want the church to give me proof that where it was going was important, and that there was a method of full accountability.

A Presbyterian pastor emphasized the necessity of written guidelines:

The most important thing needed to build the endowment has to be a promise that there will be integrity in the endowment, and you won't use it for anything it wasn't intended for, like spend the principal. You need to say what you will use the interest for. So you've got to have good guidelines—open, public guidelines. And they've got to be fair. And you really have to have a vision.

Socially responsible investing is another issue. Some people feel a responsibility for ensuring that church reserves are invested in companies consistent with their Christian mission (such as avoiding tobacco companies, breweries, or companies with a record of poor labor relations), even if that means a lower return. This was a crucial issue, for example, in the late 1980s as churches argued over the decision to invest in companies doing business in South Africa. An Episcopal priest told us of the turmoil in his congregation:

We had a huge fight over South Africa a couple of years ago. The vestry fought with each other for a year and a half over whether to divest, and then they divested by a single vote. I did not push one way or another, and I felt bad about that. I said to them, I think we should divest, but it is your decision to make. And I had several people say to me that they wanted me to be a stronger moral influence. They wanted me to tell people that this is what you have to do. I said that is not the way Anglicans work. Anglican clergy don't tell people how to behave morally. They don't tell people how to make moral decisions that are complex and difficult. And so, I felt bad about that. I felt that I was sort of waffling, but I myself waffled.

The pastors we spoke with were keenly aware that an emphasis on socially responsible investing results in a lower return. One told us of the uproar among the pastors in his denomination when the church's pension fund board decided to sell all investments in South Africa, causing the fund to earn a lower return.

An Episcopal priest recounted an ongoing dispute that he is currently embroiled in with his parish's finance committee chair whenever he advocates socially responsible investing.

Our finance chair thinks it is a terrible thing. He says, "Why don't we get the maximum?" And he takes my argument about the reserves and turns it back against me. He says we need to support the local church as much as we can, so we need to take the money and invest it at its highest return.

A Presbyterian executive perhaps best summed up the feelings of all the pastors we spoke with:

I think both considerations are valid. I think prudence says that you've been made stewards of this money and it's supposed to produce some income. But within that, I think you can make a lot of relative judgments about whether investments are more or less responsible. And a lot of decisions are going to be murky, because no corporation is pure. But I think taking into account the whole concern about social responsibility is a good thing to do.

How can the congregation deal with these multiple goals? One solution is to hire a professional to manage the investments. But even this is problematic. Who in the congregation has the expertise to monitor the professional's work? What if a congregation member is an investment professional? Should investment management be turned over to this individual? What oversight will the congregation place on one of its own members? Will the member be fired if the investments perform poorly? These are all sources of congregational conflict that reserves bring.

Problems managing reserves are real. It is worth recalling that secrecy and evasiveness existed in many Protestant churches in the past. Story after story can be heard about protective investment committees in the 1940s or 1950s. From all indications there has been increased openness and disclosure in recent years, and we believe this is important.

In summary, reserve accounts are emerging in many Christian churches. Churches that never considered creating reserves, whether for theological or practical reasons, are now reconsidering their position and are studying the issue seriously. Other churches with a long history of established reserves are struggling to make sure that invested reserve funds are placed in the proper perspective and that the tail does not wag the dog.

There is still disagreement among church leaders as to whether, overall, invested reserves are a good thing or a bad thing. In our experience much of the negative sentiment about reserves revolves not so much around their existence, but around how they are regulated and managed. The arguments against reserves are partly arguments against mismanagement of investments.

Both the donors and the recipient congregations need to know the pitfalls and the problems associated with endowments and other reserves. Churches need written guidelines. Denominations could provide a valuable service to their congregations by developing basic principles on endowment considerations such as: (a) adequate openness and communication with the members; (b) how to manage the money; (c) designating income; (d) spending or lending the principal; and so on.

The trend toward establishing and building reserve funds is probably irreversible. More church members than ever have fortunes, and many of them savor giving to endowments. Whether churches like it or not, this is an unavoidable element of stewardship.

For Reflection and Discussion

1. Which arguments for or against endowments are most persuasive to you? Why?

2. If your church has an endowment, does it have written policies for receiving, investing, and spending the money? If so, how could the policies be clarified or otherwise improved? If not, what could you do to begin putting policies in place?

3. What are your views about whether an endowment should be restricted or unrestricted? Why?

4. Do you agree or disagree that churches with endowments should invest the money in "socially responsible" companies or funds? Why?

CHAPTER 8

What Does All This Mean? Commentary and Questions

Loren B. Mead

The Difficulty of Communicating

Anyone who has reached this point in this book has been on a journey into totally unknown territory. Money, giving, stewardship, pledging, tithing, endowment—all these are familiar words to those of us who participate in religious institutions. They are words most pastors and laity use regularly in almost every one of the 350,000 congregations across the United States of America. But no one before has really looked at how these seemingly familiar words relate to each other and how they are used by different families of congregations.[1]

Indeed, the very use of these terms has been misleading, often, because they have been used in one faith community with meanings that differ from their usage in others. For years we have thought we were talking about the same thing, only to discover that these words mean quite different things to different groups. More than that, we find that the words are often not clear even within the same congregation or denomination. "Pledging," for example, is a word with rich meanings for Presbyterians and Lutherans, but "tithing" still remains slightly suspect. The opposite is true for those in the Assemblies of God. Both concepts are foreign to many Catholic laypersons. Each of these relatively familiar words carries a cultural bias when used in other families. No wonder it is not easy to be clear when we talk about giving in churches.

Another reason why it is difficult to communicate clearly about church giving patterns is that there really are two tasks—making generous people out of church members and taking care of the financing of the institution itself. The requirements for one task sometimes collide with the needs of the other task.

The book's description of the tension between "stewardship" and "fund raising" begins to explore this territory. Both "stewardship" and "fund raising" as practiced in the churches are concerned at least partly with getting the funds to support the institution. The slightly different focus of the two terms make communication difficult and sometimes confusing.

Exploring Patterns of Giving

I find the authors' brief description of the "history" of church finance provocative.[2] I have wondered why no history of the church I have ever read has dealt with the history of the economics of churches, why all discussion I have ever heard about churches and finance makes no reference to practices before the twentieth century. All those ways of paying for church that were common prior to the early twentieth century are simply not part of the conversation today.

With the thanks for the work of the authors of this book, I also wonder whether further research might be done about how finances have affected other periods of the church's life. For example, for some time I have been trying to get historians or theologians to explore my hunch that the Reformation may have been just as much about money as it was about theology. The church historians I know focus on the critical theological issues that were fought out—the relationship of grace, faith, and works. That is their territory and they are comfortable with it. But I wonder what the practical impact was when the steady, widespread income from the sale of indulgences was threatened. You can debate theology all you want, but what happens when salaries are at stake? The old folk saying may be applicable here: "They done quit preaching and started meddling."

Relishing what the researchers have already discovered, I also long for future studies that will lead us not only to greater historical perspective but also to see patterns by which other communities face funding issues—the African-American patterns of giving and those of the Hispanic-American and Asian-American congregations. How do those patterns fit or differ from the denominational patterns described here? And do the ethnic patterns of giving modify the denominational?

The other glaring need for future research is in longitudinal studies of givers: What are the lifelong or even decade-long patterns of giving? We need stories of how people become givers, how patterns of giving are established, what causes patterns to change, and how persistent givers maintain their patterns in a society that does not value selflessness.

Trust and Social Institutions

This book also points to a phenomenon in our society that has implications for churches—the lowered sense of trust people have in social institutions. That loss of credibility and trust obviously has had direct impact upon levels of giving at all levels of our church bodies. Similarly, the increased desire of many members to control how their gifts will be used is in conflict with the need of institutional leaders to have predictable income flow that can be budgeted and managed for programs and ongoing commitments.[3]

One would expect, in such a situation, strong evidence of a need for increased participatory decision making around funding issues. One looks in vain, however, for evidence that improving the participation in decision making is likely to improve the level of giving. Apparently the systems that make "top down" decisions about money issues seem to be in no better or worse shape than the systems that highly value and practice participatory decision making regarding finances. In fact, one could observe that the most participatory denominations have, in recent decades, suffered the most noticeable declines in funding.[4] The issue of trust in the system apparently has to do with much more complex dynamics than simple democratic processes.

Tension among Givers

Giving in churches is surrounded by such high-test emotional language that I found the description of four types of motivation rather freeing. The authors, by using the descriptive language that fits their disciplines, help us to make clear some distinctions and to see how different sets of motivations are at work in us and in our stewardship programming.

These descriptions get us away from the evaluative, often pejorative language people tend to use for systems other than their own.

Stewardship versus Fund Raising

Having made those distinctions, however, I feel that the authors may have overstated the difference between fund raising and stewardship. In the experience of the churches I have worked with, there is a very fuzzy relationship between stewardship and fund raising. The actual boundary is not as clear as the language of this book suggests. I find hard-nosed fund raisers in congregations using the language of stewardship, and I find stewardship advocates using the quite pragmatic tools of the fund raiser. Planning and organizing the annual stewardship campaign is carried out with genuine concern for helping people connect their giving, their pledge, or their tithe with their relationship to God and to others. But the congregation's leaders express equal concern for finding enough funds to fix the roof, pay the pastor, and send funds to important mission causes. When the campaign cranks up, it is hard to tell what is stewardship and what is fund raising. There is a tension between these concepts, but most of the people in congregations seem to genuinely believe in both. The result is bound to be some confusion.

Connectionalism

Another tension is seen in the different relationship congregations of different denominations have with their regional or national structures. The ecclesiological shorthand for this is, "How 'connectional' are they?" In this language, for example, some of the megachurches as well as congregations with loose denominational connections are not very "connectional." They are not required to follow denominational requirements or guidelines to participate in denominational mission budgets.

Other denominational systems, on the other hand, sometimes give the impression to their congregations that payment to the regional or national mission budget is a requirement—almost a tax. Sometimes, to the dismay of the denomination, people in congregations talk about the requirement as a "head tax." Still other denominations look very connectional, if not even hierarchical, but the appearance is a facade, and the bishops or executives have no teeth. Where one is on that continuum from tight to loose connectionalism, however, influences the patterns of giving and expectations within the congregations.

The Purpose of the Church

One other tension I detected that operates in the world of stewardship in churches is passionate conflict of values about the nature of the church's enterprise itself. The conflict is so passionate that it is often very difficult to deal with. Two issues seem to trigger those conflicts:

1. Is the primary purpose of the church to maintain its fabric and structure, primarily, or is it to contribute to the alleviation of human or social needs? I have stated this tension as an "either-or," which is the way it gets a conflict started in congregations, although the church has always refused to accept the starkness of this distinction. "What is the money for?" this tension asks—to take care of ourselves or to take care of those hurting around the world? Stewardship is complicated in congregations where this conundrum is set up as a conflict in which one side must win and the other lose.

2. The second area of continuing tension I find revolves around the concept of "endowment." Some church people have a severe allergy to the word; others see it as prudent management of resources. In conflict situations this tension gets expressed in "either-or" terms also, the word "endowment" is understood to refer to a specific kind of financial asset. Is the endowment just a trust fund to excuse us from responsibility, or is it a way to secure the future of the ministry of the church? Lost in the conversation between these views are the spiritual needs of those who have resources they wish to leave to the next generation and want to entrust to their church. Lost, also, is a broader understanding of the many resources that "endow" a congregation—physical and economic things like buildings, personal things like generations of families, and other important things like a congregational or denominational heritage and tradition.

How in the World Did We Get Here?

From the first pages of this book, I was struck by the difficulty people
have talking about the subject of giving to the church. What I hear in
this book is voice after voice talking very judgmentally about money in
churches—or judgmentally about people's positions about money in the
churches. Positions are black and white, good and bad. Pastor's voices
are full of pain and frustration and often a sense of inadequacy and
unpreparedness. I am not surprised that seminaries are scapegoated for
not having prepared the clergy for this part of their job. With the degree
of discomfort I hear in these pastors' voices, I am not surprised that there
is a need to blame somebody. What is interesting in the one piece of
research that has been done on the subject[5] makes it quite clear that
those who go to theological seminary have an aversion to spending time
working on issues of stewardship or financial management.[5]

More seems to be at stake. Yes, pastors have feelings of inadequacy
and unpreparedness to deal with money, but they also feel prohibited
from dealing with it. Hear some of the voices from earlier chapters of
this book:

- Clergy "fear that they'll alienate members if they push too hard."

- New technical aspects of stewardship "make many pastors feel
  inadequate."

- "When you go to people and say, 'Okay, we've got to talk about
  money,' most ministers I know are a little shy of that because they
  know that it can be a negative and confrontational subject for some
  folks. They just try to avoid it. 'Don't get into that, because when
  you get into that, it will mean conflict.'"

- Another pastor says, "I find there is a fear among pastors who don't
  want to go out and ask an individual for money, especially people
  they know. They're afraid of alienating them, of pushing them too
  far."

What we seem to have is more than a lack of training. We have,
rather, a widespread sense of pressure not to deal with money issues.

Whether this is a genuine response to outside pressure, we cannot tell. It is clear that it is a strong psychic reality for many clergy who genuinely think the pressure is real.

It is interesting how compelling the cultural images are that under-gird these feelings in clergy. The book notes the caricature of Pastor Grabadollar, presented as hilarious to a comedy audience, but obviously not very funny to the Lutheran pastor who remembers it years later. Similarly clergy remember Elmer Gantry and face a world in which there are conspicuous examples of clergy's financial excess—from the Bakkers and Swaggarts of television to the pastor (everyone seems to know one) in the next town who just bought a Cadillac.

Clergy respond to these jibes, to these cultural symbols, by internalizing the fear. Rather than speak out to give strong leadership about money and to see whether such talk does alienate people, the clergy accept the alienation as real and do not speak out. They do a preemptive strike on their own leadership, capitulating to the opposition without knowing whether the opposition is really there. The cultural taboos are internalized by the clergy and accepted as true. The clergy voluntarily step back from confrontation, responding to the anxiety within.

Clergy often come to their calling with a distinct aversion to conflict and to having to deal with money issues. Our culture seems to reinforce them in that behavior. So long as clergy are cowed and anxious in the face of money and wealth, they will remain silent about the spiritual issue that touches our culture more deeply than any other.

The more I steeped myself in this book and looked at the churches around me, the more I became convinced this behavior is the way a culture controls a challenge to itself. A money-driven culture seems to want clergy who are "safe" and "tame" when dealing with the spiritual dimension of money. This book catalogues a set of behaviors that encourage church members to talk about money in circumlocutions and in indirect discussion. The first rule of churches and money seems to be, "Obfuscate!" Congregations and denominations use confusing language to talk about what they do in stewardship. They also[6] cover up how funds are used with language that does not speak in ways that ordinary people can understand. ("Do you mean that this item called 'outreach mission in the world' is how we pay the bishop's salary?")

Ending the Conspiracy of Silence

This book is about a central reality in every congregation in this country —how it secures the financial resources to undergird its life and carry out its purposes. It is just as surely about a central spiritual issue every church member faces every day—how to deal with those gifts we have been given by God.

I believe here, for almost the first time, some straight talk is being attempted to help us out of the unhealthy collusion we have had between clergy and laity, between congregations and their denominations, between members of congregations.

If the religious institutions of the next millennium are going to be healthy and strong, they must do a far better job than they have in the past century of dealing with the financial underpinnings of religious life.

If the religious institutions of the next millennium are going to be much use to a materialistic consumer culture, they will have to speak clearly and directly to that culture where it lives. And that materialistic consumer culture lives and breathes in every member of every one of those churches. And also in every clergy person.

The conspiracy of silence that clergy and laity have allowed—if not welcomed—about the critical role of money in our spiritual lives must come to an end. Everyone who reads this sentence is one of those described by Jesus as a "ten-talent servant." Our conspiracy of silence lets us play-act as if we were all one-talent servants. It is time for that deception to end.

Dealing with church giving, stewardship, pledging, tithing, and endowments is the place to begin. They are places we must begin if we want to ensure the survival and strength of the ministry of our churches.

But those same words—giving, pledging, stewardship, tithing, endowment—are also the very places to begin the greater spiritual task— learning to live responsibly as ten-talent servants, those to whom much has been given.

For Reflection and Discussion

1. What words are most meaningful to you when you think about your own giving? Why? How might these words be misunderstood by others?

2. What ideas or information presented in this book have been most surprising to you? What has been most helpful, and why? Most challenging, and why?

3. Which of the four tensions identified by Mead (stewardship versus fund raising, connectionalism, the mission of the church, endowments) are present in your congregation? How are the tensions manifest? Which causes the most difficulty? How might you address those tensions?

4. How do you experience the pressure not to talk about money issues in your congregation? Have you ever tested those pressures to see how real they are? If so, how did you do that? What happened?

5. What could you do in your congregation to help people to break the conspiracy of silence and to begin "talking straight" about money?

NOTES

Introduction

1. C. Kirk Hadaway and David A. Roozen, *Rerouting the Protestant Mainstream: Sources of Growth and Opportunities for Change* (Nashville: Abingdon Press, 1995).

2. Loren Mead, "Financial Meltdown in the Mainline: A Paper for Discussion," (unpublished, 1996), p. 2.

3. John L. Ronsvalle and Sylvia Ronsvalle, *Behind the Stained Glass Windows: Money Dynamics in the Church* (Grand Rapids, Mich.: Baker Books, 1996).

4. Dean Hoge et al., *Money Matters: Personal Giving in American Churches* (Louisville, Ky.: Westminster John Knox Press, 1996).

5. We may note that we were interested in possible differences between men and women pastors in financial leadership. We interviewed both and discussed the topic with them, and we found general agreement that the differences are small and indistinct.

Chapter 1

1. John L. Ronsvalle and Sylvia Ronsvalle, *Beyond the Stained Glass Windows: Money Dynamics in the Church* (Grand Rapids, Mich.: Baker Books, 1996), p. 330.

2. Ronsvalle and Ronsvalle, *Beyond the Stained Glass Windows,* p. 331.

3. See Daniel Conway, ed., *The Reluctant Steward: A Report and Commentary on the Stewardship and Development Study* (Indianapolis, Ind.: Christian Theological Seminary, 1992).

4. Conway, *The Reluctant Steward*, p. 22.

5. Lee Strobel, *Inside the Mind of Unchurched Harry and Mary* (Grand Rapids, Mich.: Zondervan, 1993).

6. Strobel, *Inside the Mind*, p. 207.

7. Strobel, *Inside the Mind*, p. 209.

8. Ronsvalle and Ronsvalle, *Behind the Stained Glass Windows*, p. 150.

9. Ronsvalle and Ronsvalle, *Behind the Stained Glass Windows*, pp. 341-42.

Chapter 2

1. E. Brooks Holifield, "Toward a History of American Congregations," in James P. Wind and James W. Lewis, eds., *American Congregations*, vol. 2, (Chicago: University of Chicago Press, 1994), pp. 23-53, esp. p. 36.

2. Holifield, "Toward a History," in *American Congregations*, p. 41.

3. For example, Joan LaFollette found that Presbyterian women's organizations contributed about 18 to 20 percent of the total funds sent to the General Assembly in the 1950s and 1960s. Women's organizations' share of funds contributed to Presbyterian foreign missions in those years was about 22 to 24 percent. See Joan C. LaFollette, "Money and Power: Presbyterian Women's Organizations in the Twentieth Century" in M. Coalter, J. Mulder, and L. Weeks (eds.) in *The Organizational Revolution: Presbyterians and American Denominationalism* (Louisville, Ky.: Westminster John Knox Press, 1992), pp. 199-232.

4. Several books have recently appeared on financing in American churches. See Dean R. Hoge, et al., *Money Matters: Personal Giving in American Churches* (Louisville, Ky.: Westminster John Knox Press, 1996); John L. Ronsvalle and Sylvia Ronsvalle, *The State of Church Giving through 1993* (Champaign, Ill.: empty tomb, inc., 1995); John L. Ronsvalle and Sylvia Ronsvalle, *Behind the Stained Glass Windows: Money Dynamics in the Church* (Grand Rapids, Mich.: Baker Books, 1996); Joseph Claude Harris, *The Cost of Catholic Parishes and Schools* (Kansas City, Mo.: Sheed and Ward, 1996); Robert Wuthnow, *The Crisis in the Churches: Spiritual Malaise, Fiscal Woe* (New York: Oxford University Press, 1997).

5. From 1987 to 1989, the General Social Survey, a reliable national poll, estimated average Catholic per-family income at $32,213, Protestant income at $29,851, and Jewish income at $40,720. See Dean R. Hoge and Fenggang Yang, "Determinants of Religious Giving in American Denominations: Data from Two Nationwide Surveys," *Review of Religious Research* 36, no. 2 (December 1994): 123-48.

6. See Barry A. Kosmin and Paul Ritterband, eds., *Contemporary Jewish Philanthropy in America* (Savage, Md.: Rowman and Littlefield, 1991), p. 28.

7. Scott L. Thumma, "The Kingdom, the Power, and the Glory: The Megachurch in Modern American Society" (Ph.D. diss., Emory University, 1996), ch. 11, p. 11 and Appendix A. See also George G. Hunter III, *Church for the Unchurched* (Nashville.: Abingdon Press, 1996).

8. On Saddleback Church see Rick Warren, *The Purpose Driven Church* (Grand Rapids, Mich.: Zondervan Publishing House, 1995). On Willow Creek Community Church see Lynne Hybels and Bill Hybels, *Rediscovering Church: The Story and Vision of Willow Creek Community Church* (Grand Rapids, Mich.: Zondervan Publishing House, 1995); Lee Strobel, *Inside the Mind of Unchurched Harry and Mary* (Grand Rapids, Mich.: Zondervan Publishing House, 1993); G. A. Pritchard, *Willow Creek Seeker Services: Evaluating a New Way of Doing Church* (Grand Rapids, Mich.: Basic Books, 1996).

9. Warren, *The Purpose Driven Church*, pp. 131-35.

10. Strobel, *Inside the Mind*, p. 206.

11. Pritchard, *Willow Creek Seeker Services*, p. 25.

12. Pritchard, *Willow Creek Seeker Services*, p. 26.

13. See Ronald E. Vallet and Charles E. Zech, *The Mainline Church's Funding Crisis: Issues and Possibilities* (Grand Rapids, Mich.: Eerdmans Publishing Company, 1995).

14. Dean R. Hoge, et al., *Money Matters*, p. 43.

15. Barry A. Kosmin, "The Dimensions of Contemporary American Jewish Philanthropy," in B. Kosmin and P. Ritterband (eds.), *Contemporary Jewish Philanthropy in America* (Savage, Md.: Rowman & Littlefield, 1991), pp. 17-30, esp. p. 27.

16. See Richard G. Niemi, John Mueller, and Tom W. Smith, *Trends in Public Opinion* (New York: Greenwood Press, 1989). The *Washington Post* compiled survey trend data on trust in institutions and found a massive 51 percent decline between 1964 and 1995 in favorable re-

sponses to the question "How much of the time do you trust the government in Washington to do the right thing?" (*Washington Post*, 28 January 1996, pp. A1, A6-A7). Declines in trust in other institutions were similar but not so steep.

17. See Vallet and Zech, *The Mainline Church's Funding Crisis*; Tony Campolo, *Can Mainline Denominations Make a Comeback?* (Valley Forge, Pa.: Judson Press, 1995); C. Kirk Hadaway and David A. Roozen, *Rerouting the Protestant Mainstream* (Nashville, Tenn.: Abingdon Press, 1995).

Chapter 3

1. Kenneth E. Boulding, *The Economy of Love and Fear: A Preface to Grants Economics* (Belmont, Calif.: Wadsworth, 1973).

2. For attempts to delineate motives for gift giving, see Russ Alan Prince and Karen M. File, *The Seven Faces of Philanthropy* (San Francisco: Jossey-Bass, 1994); Gilbert E. Clary and M. Snyder, "A Functional Analysis of Altruism and Prosocial Behavior," in M. S. Clark, ed., *Review of Personality and Social Psychology*, vol. 12 (Newbury Park, Calif.: Sage, 1991), pp. 3-15.

3. See Teresa Odendahl, *Charity Begins at Home: Generosity and Self-Interest Among the Philanthropic Elite* (New York: Basic Books, 1990); Susan A. Ostrander and Paul G. Schervish, "Giving and Getting: Philanthropy as a Social Relation," in Jon Van Til, ed., *Critical Issues in American Philanthropy: Strengthening Theory and Practice* (San Francisco: Jossey-Bass, 1990), pp. 67-98; Francie Ostrower, *Why the Wealthy Give: The Culture of Elite Philanthropy* (Princeton, N.J.: Princeton University Press, 1995).

4. Teresa Odendahl, *Charity Begins at Home*, p. 37.

5. Max Weber, *The Sociology of Religion* (1922; reprinted, Boston: Beacon Press, 1963), pp. 138-39.

6. Roberta Simmons, *Gift of Life: The Effect of Organ Transplantation on Individual, Family, and Societal Dynamics* (New Brunswick, N.J.: Transaction Books, 1987).

7. See John D. Baldwin and Janice I. Baldwin, *Behavior Principles in Everyday Life*, 2d ed. (Englewood Cliffs, N.J.: Prentice-Hall, 1986).

8. Dean R. Hoge, Benton Johnson, and Donald A. Luidens, *Vanishing Boundaries: The Religion of Mainline Protestant Baby Boomers* (Louisville, Ky.: Westminster John Knox Press, 1994).

Chapter 4

1. John L. Ronsvalle and Sylvia Ronsvalle, *Behind the Stained Glass Windows: Money Dynamics in the Church* (Grand Rapids, Mich.: Baker Books, 1996), pp. 19-20, 133-35.

Chapter 5

1. James M. Greenfield, *Fund-Raising Fundamentals* (New York: John Wiley, 1994), p. 13.
2. Ronald W. Vallet, *Stepping Stones of the Steward* (Grand Rapids, Mich.: Eerdmans Publishing Company, 1989), p. 4.
3. The author of this stewardship statement is the Rev. Mark Moller-Gunderson, Executive Director, ELCA Division for Congregational Ministries, Chicago, Ill.
4. Kennon L. Callahan, *Effective Church Finances* (San Francisco: Harper Collins, 1992), pp. 14-15, 63.

Chapter 6

1. Loren Mead, "Caught in the Financial Bind: Reflections on Clergy and Money," *Congregations* 23, no. 3 (July-August 1996): 3.

Chapter 7

1. See *Survey of Endowed Presbyterian Churches* (Wilmington, Del.: National Association of Endowed Presbyterian Churches, 1995). The report is based on a survey of 142 churches with investments of $500,000 or more.
2. Alan Farnham, "The Windfall Awaiting the New Inheritors," *Fortune* 121, no. 10 (May 7, 1990): 72-78.
3. Quoted by Keith Hinson in "Inheritance Windfall May Bypass Churches," *Christianity Today*, April 7, 1997, p. 58.
4. Dean Hoge, et al., *Money Matters: Personal Giving in American Churches* (Louisville, Ky.: Westminster John Knox Press, 1996), p. 72; *Survey of Endowed Presbyterian Churches*, pp. 10-11.
5. John L. Ronsvalle and Sylvia Ronsvalle, *Behind the Stained Glass Windows: Money Dynamics in the Church* (Grand Rapids, Mich.: Baker Books, 1996), pp. 339-40.
6. See *Survey of Endowed Presbyterian Churches*, pp. 51-52.

Chapter 8

1. I must point out the obvious fact that this book stands on the shoulders of *Monday Matters: Personal Giving in American Churches* (Louisville, Ky.:Westminster John Knox, 1996), in which empirical studies of many of these issues by Hoge, Donahue, McNamara, and Zech were reported.

2. See above, chapter 2.

3. Leaders of eleven denominations who met to discuss the future of denominational systems noted one thing as both their greatest sign of hope and their greatest anxiety—the rapid increase of "designated giving."

4. See John L. Ronsvalle and Sylvia Ronsvalle, *The State of Church Giving through 1993* (Champaign, Ill.: empty tomb, inc., 1995).

5. "The Reluctant Steward" is a report cosponsored by the Christian Theological Seminary and Saint Meinrad Seminary. This 1992 document tells of a study of constituents and students at two seminaries and their attitudes toward and interest in learning about stewardship and financial management. Project director was Daniel Conway.

6. See *Patterns of Parish Leadership* (Kansas City, Mo.: Sheed and Ward, 1988). This book points out how information is kept and reported in such confusing ways that one simply cannot discover basic information about clergy costs without painstaking research.